THE GR5 TRAIL – VOSGES AND JURA

SCHIRMECK TO LAC LÉMAN, AND THE GR53

About the Authors

Les and Elizabeth Smith originally trained as a scientist and a geographer, and spent many years pursuing sensible careers. Their outdoor interests encouraged them to adopt a less secure but more flexible lifestyle, which allows more time for exploring the Scottish hills and travelling further afield.

Enthusiastic walkers and campers, they have backpacked along many long distance routes, both in the UK and more widely in Europe. Their trips often take them to less publicised areas, where a walking trail can provide an excellent way of seeing the country and meeting local people. They firmly believe that travelling and enjoying the outdoors does not depend on a generous budget.

THE GR5 TRAIL – VOSGES AND JURA

SCHIRMECK TO LAC LÉMAN, AND THE GR53

by Les and Elizabeth Smith

2 POLICE SQUARE, MILNTHORPE, CUMBRIA LA7 7PY
www.cicerone.co.uk

First edition (*Trekking in the Vosges and Jura*) 2006

Printed by KHL Printing, Singapore
A catalogue record for this book is available from the British Library.

The routes of the GR®, PR® and GRP® paths in this guide
have been reproduced with the permission of the Fédération
Française de la Randonnée Pédestre holder of the exclusive
rights of the routes. The names GR®, PR® and GRP® are registered trademarks.
© FFRP 2017 for all GR®, PR® and GRP® paths appearing in this work.

All photographs are by the author unless otherwise stated.

Acknowledgements

We would like to thank the many people we met along the route who provided
companionship and useful information. Walking these trails would be much
harder without the efforts of the many volunteers who maintain the waymarking:
to them, our thanks.

Updates to this Guide

While every effort is made by our authors to ensure the accuracy of guidebooks as
they go to print, changes can occur during the lifetime of an edition. Any updates
that we know of for this guide will be on the Cicerone website (www.cicerone.
co.uk/812/updates), so please check before planning your trip. We also advise
that you check information about such things as transport, accommodation and
shops locally. Even rights of way can be altered over time. We are always grateful
for information about any discrepancies between a guidebook and the facts on
the ground, sent by email to updates@cicerone.co.uk or by post to Cicerone,
2 Police Square, Milnthorpe LA7 7PY, United Kingdom.

Front cover: Approaching Belacker (Section 7)

CONTENTS

Map key 7
Summary map of the GR5/GR53 route 8
Route profile for the GR5/GR53 route. 9

INTRODUCTION 11
Why visit the Vosges and Jura? 11
Landscape 12
History 14
Wildlife 17
When to visit 19
Access 20
Local transport 20
Accommodation. 20
Camping. 21
Food and drink 21
What to take. 22
Maps 23
GR system and waymarking 23
Safety and health 24
Language 25
Money 25
Telephones and internet 25
Using this guide 25

THE GR53 WISSEMBOURG TO SCHIRMECK 27
Section 1   GR53 Wissembourg to Niederbronn-les-Bains 28
Section 2   GR53 Niederbronn-les-Bains to Saverne 39
Section 3   GR53 Saverne to Schirmeck 53

THE GR5 SCHIRMECK TO NYON 67
Section 4   GR5 Schirmeck to Ribeauvillé. 69
Section 5   GR5 Ribeauvillé to Mittlach 84
Section 6   GR5 Mittlach to Thann 96
Section 7   GR5 Thann to Brévilliers 107
Section 8   GR5 Brévilliers to St-Hippolyte 122
Section 9   GR5 St-Hippolyte to Villers-le-Lac. 133

Section 10 GR5 Villers-le-Lac to Les Hôpitaux-Neufs 146
Section 11 GR5 Les Hôpitaux-Neufs to Nyon 159

SHORT WALKS ALONG THE GR5/GR53 175

Appendix A   Long distance routes in the Vosges and Jura 182
Appendix B   Route summary tables 184
Appendix C   Facilities table. 186
Appendix D   Useful websites 193
Appendix E   Accommodation. 195

Map Key

══════════	road
──────────	GR5/GR53
··················	GR5/GR53 alternative route
SW1	short walk start/finish
⌇⌇⌇⌇⌇⌇⌇⌇⌇	canal
～～～	river
‒ ‒ ‒	national boundary
▢	regional park
▲	summit
△	lookout point or named rock
■	other building
○	ruin or building of historic interest
©	cave
♖	castle
⬭⬭⬭	village or town
N66	road number
◀	route direction
⊞⊞⊞⊞⊞⊞⊞⊞	railway

Contour colour key

	over 1600m
	1400-1600m
	1200-1400m
	1000-1200m
	800-1000m
	600-800m
	400-600m
	200-400m
	0-200m

Contour colour key for overview maps only

	over 2000m
	1500-2000m
	1000-1500m
	500-1000m
	200-500m
	0-200m

Summary map of the
GR5/GR53 route
through the
Vosges and Jura

N

0   50 km

GR53 ··········
GR5 ——
Regional
Parks

Northern Vosges
Regional Park

Ballons des Vosges
Regional Park

Haut-Jura
Regional Park

Lorraine

Alsace

VOSGES

Wissembourg
Niederbronn-
les-Bains
Saverne
STRASBOURG
Schirmeck
Ribeauvillé
Colmar
Mittlach
Thann
Mulhouse
Belfort
Brévilliers
Héricourt
GERMANY
River Rhine
BASEL

FRANCE
River Doubs
St-Hippolyte
Villers-le-Lac
Franche-Comté
J U R A
Les Hôpitaux-Neufs
Mouthe
Nyon
Lake Geneva
GENEVA

SWITZERLAND

FRANCE   Vosges   GERMANY
                            AUSTRIA
         Jura
      SWITZERLAND
                   ITALY

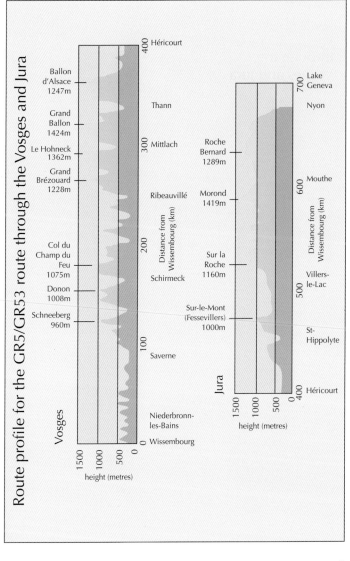

Route profile for the GR5/GR53 route through the Vosges and Jura

Vosges

height (metres)

1500 1000 500 0

Distance from Wissembourg (km)

400 — Héricourt

Thann

300 — Mittlach

Ribeauvillé

200 —

Schirmeck

100 —

Saverne

Niederbronn-les-Bains

0 — Wissembourg

Ballon d'Alsace 1247m

Grand Ballon 1424m

Le Hohneck 1362m

Grand Brézouard 1228m

Col du Champ du Feu 1075m

Donon 1008m

Schneeberg 960m

Jura

height (metres)

1500 1000 500 0

Distance from Wissembourg (km)

700 — Lake Geneva

Nyon

Mouthe

600 —

Villers-les-Lac

500 —

St-Hippolyte

400 — Héricourt

Roche Bernard 1289m

Morond 1419m

Sur la Roche 1160m

Sur-le-Mont (Fessevillers) 1000m

9

Cascade du Nideck (Section 3)

INTRODUCTION

Vosges landscape from Le Grand Ballon (Section 6)

WHY VISIT THE VOSGES AND JURA?

Imagine a landscape of rolling hills and deeply cut gorges, of ruined castles, villages with half-timbered houses, and a network of footpaths weaving through forests. All this and more can be seen in the Vosges and Jura. In some places it is possible to walk for hours in peaceful solitude, while in others, lively local towns provide a choice of distractions. This book describes a walking route linking this rich variety of landscapes, using well-marked paths to cross a slice of France.

The whole region has an excellent footpath system, well within the capabilities of any moderately fit person. These mountains are ideal for walkers, the summits being of modest height, and panoramic views make the breathless ascents worthwhile. The whole walk described in this book is a substantial undertaking, needing five or six weeks to complete, but even walking a few days along the route introduces you to some of these enchanting places.

In the north of the region the Northern Vosges is a land of tranquil forests where people are few and wildlife is undisturbed. Nature has eroded the sandstone here to leave spectacular rock pinnacles, often with the half-forgotten ruins of a medieval castle perched precariously above the treetops.

11

In the Central and Southern Vosges the forests have their own surprises. The enigmatic ruins of the Mur Païen and the nearby convent of Mont Ste-Odile are shrouded in legend and mystery (Section 4). Footpaths lead through the age-old winegrowing towns and villages on the edge of the Alsace Plain and up through the trees to open summit pastures. There is so much to discover here – do you linger to savour the charm of old Alsace, with its cobbled lanes and half-timbered houses, or do you press on up to the windswept hilltops, where the view over the patchwork plain extends out to the distant Alps?

Further south the limestone of the Jura lends its own unique character to the landscape. Isolated lookout points give wide views over the seemingly endless blanket of trees below. Elsewhere, rivers have cut down through the limestone to produce impressive gorge scenery, with narrow defiles leading between rocky crags. Joux Castle, surely one of the most stunningly sited strongholds in all of France, stands guard over one such narrow rocky cleft (Section 10). The rivers can form gentle backwaters where trout linger in shaded pools, or they can have more dramatic moods – at Saut du Doubs the thunder of rushing water can be heard long before the waterfall comes into sight (Section 9).

Special mention should be made of the wall of cliffs by Le Mont d'Or (Section 11), where the clifftop path

provides magnificent vantage points over the expanse of the Swiss Jura.

This book is a practical guide to the principal north–south walking route through this varied landscape, along the GR5/GR53. The 687.5km (427-mile) waymarked path traverses the entire length of the Vosges, and then climbs up onto the plateau of the Haut-Jura before dropping down to Nyon on the shores of Lake Geneva (Lac Léman). The GR5 is one of the great walking routes across Europe, crossing the continent from the Dutch coast to the Mediterranean, and the route described here is the central section (518km), from the Vosges down to Lake Geneva. In addition, the GR53 in the Northern Vosges (169.5km) is described as an offshoot of the GR5 that allows walkers to complete the entire chain of the Vosges. These quiet hills of the Northern Vosges are often overlooked by visitors, yet have become a personal favourite of ours.

LANDSCAPE

In the Northern Vosges the low, rounded hills are mostly formed from eroded sandstone, but in places where it is more resistant to erosion, prominent rocky outcrops remain. These isolated high points make obvious defensive sites, and the sandstone castles built on them can look like extensions of the rock itself. Further south in the Vosges this layer of sandstone has been eroded away completely to reveal gneiss and

Dames des Entreportes (Section 10)

granite, harder rock which makes up the higher land, the Ballons des Vosges (Sections 5 to 7), with massive, flat-topped summits and ridges. The east face of the range, which follows the fault line of the Rhine Valley, is steeper than the west and in places forms a line of impressive cliffs. Glaciation has left its mark on these hills. Valleys were widened in some places to form massive, bowl-shaped cirques which are now the sites of glacial lakes. A series of such lakes, including Lac Blanc and Lac Noir, lies just below the cliffs.

Above the forest, the tops of the hills are open pasture. The very highest pastures are naturally clear of trees as a result of exposure, but others have traditionally been kept clear by grazing. Below the forest, the lower slopes to the south and east are clothed in vineyards. Winemaking in Alsace dates back many centuries, and has given rise to a whole string of inviting little villages in the valleys.

South of the Vosges a mix of sedimentary rocks forms the low land around Belfort, where the GR5 goes through areas of farming and forestry.

Just south of Vandoncourt the striking rock arch of Pont Sarrazin (Section 8) is the first unmistakable sign that the path has reached the limestone that forms the basis of the scenery for the rest of the route to Lake Geneva. The limestone of the Jura creates a landscape distinct from the Vosges. Rivers have cut deep gorges and often flow underground

through caverns. One of the highlights of the GR5 is where it follows the River Doubs as it flows through a series of wooded gorges along the Swiss frontier (Section 9).

The GR5 then climbs onto the high plateau of the Jura where the limestone extends to great depths. Folded by earth movements and split by faults, the whole region was scoured by ice so that the resulting plateau is far from flat, instead forming an undulating landscape at about 1000m, now largely covered by forest. Elevated lookout points such as Roche Bernard give expansive views.

The path leaves the plateau soon after crossing into Switzerland and descends quite steeply, the final few kilometres crossing the belt of flat fields surrounding Lake Geneva.

HISTORY

In 58BC Caesar led the Romans into battle just south of the Vosges and the Romans were to remain there for a further four centuries. Many towns can date their origins to this period; Nyon on Lake Geneva was founded by the Romans. Roads were built through some of the Vosges passes (Saverne and Donon) and a stretch of the GR5 dropping towards Nyon (Section 11) follows an old cobbled track that dates back to this time.

The eighth and ninth centuries saw the spread of Christianity and the founding of several abbeys, including that at Wissembourg.

The GR53 and GR5 through the Vosges lie for the most part in the region of Alsace, but south from the Ballon d'Alsace to the Swiss border the route runs through Franche-Comté. These regions have very different histories. Alsace, in particular, has a heritage that is part French and part German, and an overview of the various border changes helps to put the region's identity into perspective.

Roman rule collapsed early in the fifth century and Alsace was invaded by the Alemanni from across the Rhine. The Alemannic language of these invaders was related to German, differing substantially from the language of the Franks, and although French is now spoken throughout Alsace, local dialects derived from this early Alemannic still thrive.

After the death of Charlemagne in 814 the land to the west became France and was separated from the German-speaking lands further east. In 870 it was agreed by treaty that Alsace should be joined to the German states to the east, and Alsace was to remain a part of this German confederation until 1648.

The region initially prospered, but by the 13th century central control was lacking and local landowners took advantage of the situation, vying with each other for power. Alsace became a mosaic of tiny 'states', and a consequence of this can be seen in the Northern Vosges today, where 30 castles, most of them now ruined, lie within the boundaries of the regional park: the GR53 passes a good selection of these strongholds.

Freundstein Castle (Section 6)

World War I lines at Hartmannswillerkopf (Section 6)

By the end of the 16th century prosperity was returning, with silver mines and wine production generating wealth in the region, but the outbreak of the Thirty Years War in 1618 brought a period of turmoil. The treaty that finally ended this conflict transferred significant parts of Alsace to France, and full integration followed, so that by 1697 the Rhine was declared to be the official French border.

Alsace was to remain a part of France until the Franco-Prussian War of 1870–71, when invading Prussian forces won a major battle near Wissembourg. Alsace was ceded to the German Reich and the ridge of the Vosges became the new Franco–German border. Old frontier stones from this era run alongside the GR5 (Section 5).

Early in World War I, major battles were fought in the Vosges at Le Linge and Hartmannswillerkopf, and trenches have survived to the present day. The GR5 passes close to these old front lines on two occasions (Sections 5 and 6).

German defeat saw Alsace pass back into French hands in 1918, but it was an uneasy peace. After the invasion in 1940, the Germans considered Alsace to be a true part of the Reich, not part of occupied France; many of the men were conscripted into the German army and sent to the Russian front. Alsace was retaken by the French during the winter of 1944–45.

To the south of Alsace the region that now forms Franche-Comté also has its origins in the same confederation of Germanic states, although this Germanic heritage is less visible in Franche-Comté today. As early as 1295 the region passed into French control, and there followed a period as part of an autonomous Burgundy.

From 1493 to 1635 Franche-Comté was a Spanish possession, although Spain had little effect on day-to-day life, and during this period France still laid claim to the region, making several attempts to annex it. French control was finally established in 1678 and Franche-Comté has remained a part of France ever since. While the lower lands around Belfort and Montbéliard have attracted industry and a dense population, the more exposed uplands of the Jura have always been sparsely populated.

WILDLIFE

The wide variety of habitats in the Vosges and Jura supports a wealth of wildlife. Although largely wooded, the region also has open highlands, gorges, river flood plains, lakes and wetlands, giving scope for many different plants and animals to thrive.

In the fields and vineyards at the edge of the plain, storks, the emblem of Alsace and once a common sight, had become alarmingly scarce, but now, thanks to captive-breeding programmes and other conservation efforts, the decline has been reversed. There is a good chance of seeing these elegant birds close to the GR5, particularly in the region of Ribeauvillé (Sections 4 and 5).

Rising into the hills, the extensive woodland cover provides shelter throughout for wild boar, with especially high numbers in the undisturbed corners of the Northern Vosges. Often the only sign that boar are nearby is the sound of something large but unseen crashing headlong through the undergrowth. Roe and red deer are to be found in the woods, but they slip away without creating such a commotion. The trees also provide shelter for red squirrel, often a much darker form than found in the UK. Dormice, beech marten, pine marten and wild cat are all present, but you need to be lucky to see them. The same goes for lynx, which were reintroduced into parts of Switzerland and spread to France from there, but numbers are low.

The woodlands attract a variety of bird species, although it is not always easy to get good views among the trees. The black woodpecker,

Storks on an Alsace rooftop

largest of the European woodpeckers, advertises its presence by characteristically loud drumming, or you may hear the raucous call of nutcrackers, large brown crows that inhabit conifer woods. The capercaillie, largest of the European grouse, breeds in the forests of the Vosges and Jura, but this shy bird is rarely seen, despite its size. One bird that may attract attention is the golden oriole. Its loud flutey call carries through the forest, with just a glimpse now and again of a yellow-and-black bird flying from tree to tree. The song of the nightingale can also commonly be heard in early summer, usually in lowland scrub. The woods also play host to Tengmalm's owl, goshawk and firecrest.

The rich growth of small plants can be very attractive in areas of more open woodland, with periwinkle and aconites, and sweetly scented lily-of-the-valley and daphne. Bilberries too are common, and the annual harvest of berries is used to make tarte aux myrtilles, a popular local dish in the Vosges.

The edge of the forests up around the tree-line is favoured grazing for chamois. These small, goat-like animals with black-and-white-striped faces are native to various parts of Europe and were introduced to the Vosges in 1956. Since then they have maintained good numbers in the region of the Ballons. They tend to seek cover during the day, so early morning and late evening are the best times to see them, with the eastern slope below Le Hohneck a good place to go looking (Section 5). Chamois are also found quite widely in the Jura, particularly near Le Mont d'Or

Wild boar are common in the Northern Vosges

Gentians on Le Mont d'Or (Section 11)

(Section 11) and on the slopes around Joux Castle (Section 10).

Out of the forests, in the upland regions, there is a chance to see larger birds of prey, including golden eagle, buzzard and kite, and the sandstone outcrops of the Vosges and the rocky cliffs of the Jura provide excellent habitat for the peregrine falcon.

On open pastures the yellow gentian is common. This broad-leaved, yellow-flowered plant, often several feet high, is found throughout the region, and extracts made from the roots are still commercially important for making liqueurs and herbal medicines (Section 11). The yellow daisy-like flowers of arnica are also collected for medicines, and it is common in some areas of the Vosges. Above the tree-line a range of Alpine plants can be found, with pasque

flower, wild narcissus, martagon lily and globe flower giving a delightful splash of colour in season.

WHEN TO VISIT

The altitude and inland position of the region result in summers that are hot, but not generally too hot for walking, and winters with snow cover typically from about November to the beginning of April. Unless you are equipped for winter walking it is better not to attempt the higher sections during this time. During the main holiday period, from mid-July to the end of August, popular centres can be busy. A dry spell in summer may be followed by a rainier autumn, but the glowing colours of the turning leaves and the bright, crisp, frosty mornings can make autumn a delightful time to visit.

19

ACCESS

The nearest major airports are Strasbourg, Geneva and Basel, but it is also worth checking flights to nearby German destinations. TGV express trains from Paris serve Strasbourg, Mulhouse, Basel, Belfort and Geneva. By road, Strasbourg is about 650km (400 miles) from Calais.

Taking the section start points in order, Wissembourg, Niederbronn-les-Bains, Saverne and Schirmeck are all accessible using French railways (SNCF). Ribeauvillé no longer has a rail station, but is easily accessed by getting the train to Sélestat, then using the regular buses which link to the train service. For Mittlach, head for the rail station at nearby Metzeral, then complete the journey on foot (3km), or use the infrequent local buses.

Thann and Héricourt (for Brévilliers) are both served by rail stations, but further south, as the route crosses the Jura, access becomes more tricky. St-Hippolyte can be accessed from the rail station at Montbéliard, using Ligne B of the Mobidoubs local bus service. Villers-le-Lac is no longer served by a bus service, and the nearest train stations are Morteau in France, 7km away, or Le Locle in Switzerland (8km). The road from Morteau to Villers-le-Lac can be busy, and a taxi might now be the best way to access the town. Further south, Les Hôpitaux-Neufs has no rail station, but currently has a connecting bus (run by SNCF) linking the station at Frasne with the town. The final section end at Nyon is on the Swiss rail network.

LOCAL TRANSPORT

Local bus services are sparse, and often infrequent where they do exist. The sections of the route through the Jura are particularly poorly served, so if possible, it is better to walk sections 9 and 10 together. If doing part of the route, starting/finishing from a point on the rail network eases the arrangements.

ACCOMMODATION

The area has a wide range of hotels, although those in mountain resorts may be geared more towards the skiing season. *Chambres d'hôtes* are rooms in private houses, similar to bed and breakfast. When planning a trip it is a good idea to check the regional and local tourist office websites (Appendix D). Local tourist offices can answer questions about accommodation in their own area and can generally make bookings.

Gîtes d'étapes, which provide inexpensive accommodation for walkers, are common along the route. Most of them simply provide dormitories, although some offer almost hotel-like facilities, with meals and private rooms. (Note that a gîte d'étape is not the same as a *gîte rural*, which is not usually available for single nights.) There are also occasional hostels, either Youth Hostels or privately run.

Refuges (mountain huts) also provide inexpensive dormitory accommodation, but making use of them is not always straightforward as many have very restricted opening periods. Where such refuges are run by walking and skiing clubs they are often open continuously only during the high season, or may be available for group bookings only or reserved for club members.

Finally, *abris* (shelters) may have little more than walls and a roof – useful for anyone caught out in bad weather. Note that the many *fermes-auberges* in the Vosges – farms offering simple meals based on local produce – do not usually offer accommodation.

CAMPING

Camping is popular in France and most campsites provide good facilities at a reasonable cost, but some are only open for a limited period. Comprehensive lists of campsites are available from tourist office websites. Wildcamping is not a right in France and different communes have different regulations. Outside restricted areas, discreetly pitching overnight may be possible, provided it is well away from roads and houses.

FOOD AND DRINK

In Alsace the German style of cooking is seen in the popularity of pork, especially sausages, and dishes such as *choucroute* (based on sauerkraut). *Kugelhopf* is a distinctive ring-shaped

Tarte aux myrtilles

A ferme-auberge in the Vosges

cake, and *tarte aux myrtilles* is made with the bilberries common on the hillsides of the Vosges.

The Jura has been famous for smoked meats since Roman times. The local products to look out for are sausages and hams, trout from the Doubs, and snails. Both the Vosges and the Jura have fine local cheeses and wines – Alsace is well known for its white wines, and the yellow wine of the Jura is particularly unusual.

Not every village has a shop, so a little forward planning of food purchases is required in some places, and you may have to carry food for a day or two. Be aware that many shops close for an extended lunch-time, which can cause considerable delay, but many, particularly bakeries, are open early in the morning. When buying meals there is a wide choice,

from village bars to restaurants. A set meal, usually of local produce, can be bought at one of the many fermes-auberges to be found in the Vosges.

WHAT TO TAKE

Although the route does not involve any scrambling or climbing, some sections are rough and exposed, so good footwear and waterproofs are essential, and a hat and sunscreen are wise precautions. The basic walking tools of maps and compass, first aid kit, torch and water bottle are necessities.

For other packing requirements, much depends on accommodation and eating preferences. If using the many hotels and chambres d'hôtes along the route, little is required other than changes of clothing and personal items. If depending on gîtes d'étapes and hostels, add a sleeping bag. The cheapest and most flexible way of travelling is with a lightweight tent – even if you are not planning to camp every night, a tent gives an alternative if accommodation is a problem. A lightweight stove and utensils are worth considering.

Backpackers will be well aware that trips are all the more enjoyable if pack weight is kept down, so ruthlessly weed out any non-essentials at the packing stage. If camping, remember that many French campsites have laundry rooms, so there is no need to carry too many changes of clothes.

MAPS

Relevant maps are listed at the beginning of each route section, and possible stockists are in Appendix D.

Four sheets of the IGN 1:100,000 (TOP100) series cover the route (Nos 112, 122, 137, 143). These maps are good for planning and in conjunction with this book can be used for route-finding, as GR paths are marked.

The IGN 1:75,000 (TOP75) maps are ideal for walkers, and cover the Vosges, but only part of the Jura, (Nos 012, 027, 028). The Club Vosgien has produced maps of the Vosges at 1:50,000, but other than these, IGN maps at 1:50,000 are not currently available for the area of the route. IGN 1:25,000 maps (TOP25) are available, these are very detailed and a large number would be needed to cover the whole route.

The maps in this guide are not meant to be sufficient for navigation – more detailed mapping information is recommended. The main place names and features on the sketch maps are shown in **bold** type in the route descriptions.

GR SYSTEM AND WAYMARKING

The GR5 and GR53 are part of an excellent network of long distance footpaths in France, the Grandes Randonnées. Waymarking of GRs is generally with a standard system of marks. A red and white rectangle (white above red) confirms the route. A cross formed by a diagonal red line crossed out by a diagonal white line is used to indicate 'incorrect route'. This system is used for the GR5 in the Jura, but the Vosges is an exception. Here, footpaths were waymarked before the nationwide system was developed, and the GR53 and the Vosges section of the GR5 are both waymarked with red rectangles.

Problems can arise where different routes intersect, for example, in the Jura, the GTJ (Grand Traversée du Jura) and the GR5 both use red and white waymarks. Waymarking is done by volunteers, and the standard is usually high. However, GR routes do change from time to time, either temporarily or permanently.

Once in Switzerland the waymarking changes to yellow diamonds. These apply to all footpaths, and this short section of the GR5 is not distinctly

Doubs Gorge (Section 9)

marked. The route is followed by looking out for the regular signboards with directions to particular places.

SAFETY AND HEALTH

UK citizens should currently obtain a European Health Insurance Card before leaving home; this entitles you to the same services as French citizens, although visits to doctors or hospitals are not completely free. In addition, purchasing suitable insurance is recommended, particularly for non-EU citizens. Another valuable source of advice and treatment of minor ailments is the *pharmacie* (chemist's shop).

Vipers are present in the area so keep a lookout, especially when among vegetation. Unfriendly dogs might also be a problem, although we have never been troubled. In the

unlikely event of snake or dog bites, seek medical advice. The walker should also be aware of the risk of contracting Lyme disease from tick bites. Current recommendations are to check for ticks at the end of the day, completely remove any that you find, and seek advice if inflammation or other symptoms develop.

Another possible hazard in France is hunting, and walkers should be aware of the possibility of shooting in the vicinity, particularly during the autumn season.

Your own first aid kit should provide treatment for foreseeable minor problems. In addition, a survival sack or lightweight tent could prove invaluable if injured, caught out by bad weather or benighted in the hills. The likelihood of weather problems can be reduced, but not eliminated, by checking the weather forecast (*la météo*), which can be found in tourist offices or newspapers.

Over-enthusiasm at the planning stage can cause problems too. Experienced walkers will already know their own capabilities, but if you are new to long distance walking some trial days before setting off (with a full pack) might help. To enjoy the walk it is really important to keep your bag as light as possible. The first few days can be the hardest, so it is a good idea not to attempt too much at the start.

If the worst does happen, in France the emergency services can be contacted by phoning 15 (medical help), 17 (police), or 18 (fire brigade), or 112, the general (multilingual) European emergency number.

Enjoyment of the outdoors will always involve risk, and it is the responsibility of each walker to look after their own safety.

LANGUAGE

Visitors do need some basic French, even if this is just provided by a phrase book. German is commonly understood in Alsace, where although the local people are fluent French speakers, many also speak Elsässisch, the Alsatian language.

MONEY

Cash-withdrawal facilities are more frequent in the larger towns. A walker on the Jura section of the GR5 will find it useful to have some Swiss francs as well as euros.

TELEPHONES AND INTERNET

Mobile phone coverage is substantial but incomplete within the Vosges and Jura, and coverage maps can be found on the internet. Most public telephones require a credit/debit card or a pre-paid card. International dialling codes are 0044 (UK), 0033 (France), and 0041 (Switzerland).

Internet cafés are scarce, but many public libraries provide internet access, and wifi is available quite widely in cafés, railway stations and other public places.

USING THIS GUIDE

We have divided the route into 11 sections of various lengths, and have tried to arrange section ends at places accessible by public transport. The outline at the beginning of each section gives an overview, with highlights of what you can expect to see and comments on walking conditions. If you are only planning to walk part of the route, these outlines may help you choose between sections. Some suggestions for where you might make overnight stops are included, although doubtless you will have your own accommodation preferences. Each section includes a sketch map and details of the relevant topographical map.

For practical planning of the walk a list of facilities available on

Traditional houses in Andlau, Alsace (Section 4)

the route can be found in Appendix C. This table lists possibilities for refreshment, or where to break your walk, and intervening distances. These possibilities are not exhaustive, but we have tried to include all the budget accommodation (campsites and gîtes) likely to be useful. We have also made a special effort to identify accommodation on the more isolated stretches of the route. Up-to-date information can be obtained from tourist offices and the internet, and we recommend that you use these sources to supplement this guide. Be aware that village shops may close, and restaurants and hotels cover a range of prices.

Contact information for accommodation can be found in Appendix E and tourist offices can be found in

Appendix D. Hotel details are not given for places with their own tourist office (where there is usually a choice of hotels). In most cases a telephone number is listed, but where refuges are not permanently manned we have, where possible, listed an appropriate website for up-to-date contact information.

The detailed route description is divided into shorter subsections, each with an indication of distance and approximate walking time, assuming a fairly moderate walking pace. Note that distances have been assessed in kilometres, and where equivalent mileages are shown, these have been rounded and so are approximate.

The guide also gives a brief overview of some of the other long distance routes in the Vosges and Jura.

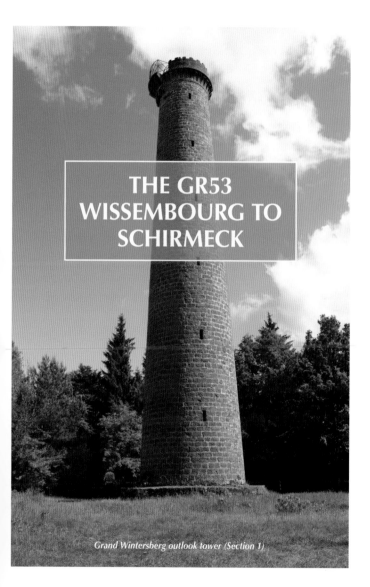

THE GR53
WISSEMBOURG TO
SCHIRMECK

Grand Wintersberg outlook tower (Section 1)

SECTION 1
GR53 WISSEMBOURG
TO NIEDERBRONN-LES-BAINS

Obersteinbach

The small town of Wissembourg, with its timber-framed medieval houses, makes a pleasant starting-off point; the buildings crowding together along the River Lauter to give the old quarter a picture-postcard appearance.

Most of the route from here to Niederbronn-les-Bains is through woodland. The hills are always relatively low, the highest point being 580m. However, as the path follows a succession of hills and valleys, in total there is a good deal of climbing to be done. The high point at the lookout tower at Wintersberg gives views over the Black Forest and the vast undulating forests of the Vosges.

What is remarkable about this section of the walk is the succession of castle ruins passed on the way, many of them taking advantage of the isolated sandstone crags that are characteristic of the Northern Vosges. Fleckenstein Castle is perhaps the most visited, its substantial walls standing on a high pinnacle close to the German border. The GR passes close to at least eight other castles before reaching Niederbronn-les-Bains, and there are several more a few kilometres distant. Among them the ruins of Loewenstein and Froensbourg are worth special mention, as both are in spectacularly elevated locations.

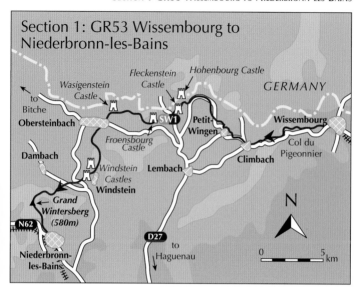

The Northern Vosges is never overwhelmed by visitors, so this first section of the route promises an interesting and relatively undisturbed walk.

A strong walker could complete this section in two days, but this would start the whole journey with a very long day, and there is much to see en route. We suggest a half-day's walk to reach one of the hotels at Climbach, then an easy day would reach Obersteinbach, with another very manageable day completing the section.

SECTION SUMMARY TABLE			
Start	Distance	Ascent/Descent	Time
Wissembourg	8.5km (5 miles)	350m/170m	2hr 40min
Climbach	9km (5.5 miles)	180m/160m	2hr 45min
Fleckenstein Castle	3km (2 miles)	180m/240m	1hr
Froensbourg Castle	7.5km (4.5 miles)	50m/110m	2hr 15min
Obersteinbach	5.5km (3.5 miles)	270m/180m	1hr 45min
Windstein	7.5km (4.5 miles)	360m/110m	2hr 45min
Grand Wintersberg	4km (2.5 miles)	0m/400m	1hr 25min

SECTION 1
Wissembourg to Niederbronn-les-Bains

Start	Wissembourg
Distance	45km (28 miles)
Maps	IGN TOP100 sheet 112; TOP75 sheet 027; Club Vosgien 1:50,000 sheet 2/8

Wissembourg to Climbach, 8.5km (5 miles), 2hr 40min
Hotels, restaurants, cafés and shops in Wissembourg; shelter on Scherhol; refuge at Col du Pigeonnier; hotel/restaurants and bakery in Climbach.

The GR53 starts from the railway station in **Wissembourg**. Turn left along the road, following red rectangle waymarks and continue past a roundabout and up the D77. Fork right along Boulevard Clemenceau (D334). The GR53 soon leaves to the right along a footpath, with the river and town wall to the right.

> The River Lauter divides into several channels to flow through **Wissembourg**, giving the old quarter a unique atmosphere. Considerable stretches of the town wall still survive, and surrounding streets are lined with handsome half-timbered buildings. The local museum, the Musée Westercamp, is itself situated in two fine 16th-century houses. As in the rest of Alsace, summer visitors will find buildings festooned with flowers, with the gardens in the centre of town adding to the colourful scene.

A footbridge crosses the river to the right, and a short diversion here reaches the picturesque older quarter of Wissembourg. The GR53 takes the path to the left, climbs up to the road and turns right. Turn left up Rue du Château d'Eau, then left again almost immediately towards Col du Pigeonnier. Follow left, uphill, on a more major road, until a waymark indicates a right turn up a track at the edge of town.

Continue uphill towards a mast, then go left at a T-junction, and right at a fork. Stay with this track for about 15min as it climbs gently to reveal a broad view over Wissembourg, then turn right, following a footpath that runs parallel to a road for over 1km.

At the parking area opposite the Maison Forestière Scherhol, turn right, then almost immediately left up the Sentier Edouard Ditenbeck. This soon reaches the remains of a *redoute*, a defensive earthwork dating back to the war of the Spanish Succession.

The GR53 crosses an adjacent parking area, heading for Scherhol Sommet, still accompanied by the bank and ditch of the old defensive system. Keep on the well-signed woodland path, turning left along a vehicle track and following the major path to the Scherhol junction.

Take the left-hand path, which leads past another embankment-and-ditch defensive work and an unlocked Club Vosgien shelter to reach the **Col Du Pigeonnier** refuge. Opening times are restricted, but there is an open shelter at the rear and accessible drinking water.

Climbach

Below the refuge the GR53 takes the Sentier Robert Redslob, signposted to Climbach. This descends through the trees, turning off sharply left almost immediately to head downhill. After about 15min it joins a vehicle track. Turn left, then when another track comes in from the right, follow it ahead. In another 15min, turn right along the road into **Climbach**.

Climbach to Fleckenstein Castle, 9km (5.5 miles), 2hr 45min
Restaurant in Petit-Wingen; café at Fleckenstein Castle.

Turn right up Rue de la Hardt, and at the end of the road follow the footpath tending left along the edge of a meadow and through woods to reach a road. The route turns left for a short distance, and then leaves to the right. At the far side of this stretch of woods, turn left down a farm track into the little village of **Petit-Wingen**, where the GR53 turns right by the restaurant. Follow the road up beyond the village and then, where it takes a sharp left turn, leave by a track to the right and very soon fork left onto a more minor track.

The route drops down to cross a stream, diverts briefly left along a lane, then takes a track up the hillside to the right. Continue to the Étang du Heinbach, then follow to the left of the *étang* (small lake) climbing steadily.

After the climb levels off, look for a track to the right and follow this down to a fork, where the route carries on downhill to Col du Litschhof, beside an open-fronted shelter. ◀ Take the middle vehicle track on the far side of the road, then leave by a footpath to the right, towards **Hohenbourg Castle** and **Loewenstein Castle**. This crosses one small track and goes quite steeply uphill before emerging onto a more level track below the castle rock. Turn left and continue uphill to Col du Hohenbourg.

The crag of Loewenstein Castle lies just ahead.

The GR53 goes to the left here, but a short detour reaches the ruins of **Hohenbourg and Loewenstein castles**, two of the castles which make the Northern Vosges special. To visit them, take the footpath to the right, then immediately fork right along the red/white/red waymarked path. The scant remains of Loewenstein are spectacularly sited on a promontory, and Hohenbourg lies just along the ridge.

Returning to Col du Hohenbourg and the GR53, go downhill, and fork right, to reach the visitor centre in front of **Fleckenstein Castle**.

Fleckenstein Castle to Froensbourg Castle, 3km (2 miles), 1hr
Fleckenstein campsite (1km off route).

The GR53 carries on past the entrance to the castle, and drops to the left to follow a well-made footpath, with the castle rock up to the right. After a few minutes the route forks right to reach the D925 (Fleckenstein campsite is 1km off-route to the left). Cross the road and pass the end of an étang. At a choice of four paths, do not take the sharp left, but the second path that turns towards the left, as waymarked. This climbs steadily, crossing two tracks

Froensbourg Castle, carved into the sandstone

then turning left along a third for a short distance before leaving to the right.

Continue along this level track, but after about 25min, look out for a narrow path to the left dropping down through trees to **Froensbourg Castle**. It may look inaccessible, but narrow pathways along the rockface and a fixed ladder allow you to explore the site.

Froensbourg Castle to Obersteinbach,
7.5km (4.5 miles), 2hr 15min
Hotels, gîte and restaurants in Obersteinbach.

Take the narrow footpath on from the castle, zigzagging uphill to join a broad track. Turn left and after only a short distance look out for a path to the right. This climbs up by a sandstone outcrop then rises, steeply at first, and emerges onto a vehicle track where the GR53 continues to the left.

Within minutes, leave by a footpath to the left, to reach a more major path. Follow this uphill to the right to Col de Hichtenbach, where there is a small shelter. Take the track left, signposted to Zigeunerfels, uphill to reach a crossroads. Go straight on, then leave the track by a substantial footpath to the right, signposted to Wasigenstein.

Turn left at a T-junction towards Zigeunerfels and follow this level track, but within 5min watch out for a footpath to the left. This passes the striking sandstone pillars of Zigeunerfels, then drops down to rejoin the track. Almost immediately, turn right to reach a road.

Cross over, and take the footpath which follows alongside the road for a few minutes, then rejoins adjacent to Klingenfels rock. Leave the road by a footpath into the forest, and almost immediately, at a junction with other trails, turn right and continue to **Wasigenstein Castle**, just off-route. This is another stark ruin perched on a sandstone crag, now partially hidden by trees.

From the castle retrace your steps, fork right towards Obersteinbach, then carry on downhill, crossing a junction. Keep following the waymarks across pastureland to join the end of a lane, which leads into **Obersteinbach**.

Klingenfels rock

**Obersteinbach to Windstein,
5.5km (3.5 miles), 1hr 45min**
Hotel/restaurant and chambres d'hôtes in Windstein.

Cross the main road and carry straight on, passing the
gîte d'étape. Turn right, up Rue de la Glockengrube, and
follow this out of the village and across some pasture.

WILD BOAR

Pastures and forest floors in this area often contain obviously churned-up
patches where wild boar have been rooting for food or wallowing in mud.
Boar are common in the forests of the Northern Vosges and popular quarry
for huntsmen. Walkers rarely get a good view of these animals, which are
most active at night, and if disturbed are usually quick to move away. They
may hold their ground occasionally, particularly if they have piglets to protect,
and the wisest course then is to retreat, as a boar, standing a metre high at the
shoulder and weighing in the region of 300kg, is a formidable beast.

Enter woods, and follow the path ahead to a junction in a clearing. Take the small footpath ahead, signposted towards the ruins of Windstein, and when this meets a track, turn right to Col du Wittschloessel.

The route of the GR53 from here as far as Grand Wintersberg uses a multitude of forest tracks and paths. The route description sounds complicated, but waymarking is good and the route is not difficult to follow.

Go straight over the junction at the col, take the left-hand path uphill, then the lower, right-hand path at a fork. When the footpath emerges onto a forest track, turn left to Col du Wineckerthal. Take a footpath opposite then turn right almost immediately onto another track. At a broad fork go left, and then at the next fork, turn right.

On reaching Col du Petit Grueneberg turn left, then immediately take a footpath to the right, up into the woods. This path hairpins up to join a track and the GR53 leaves by an uphill path almost opposite. The route skirts the top of the hill and then drops down to meet another track. Turn right to pass the sign at Wassersteine.

Soon afterwards, follow waymarks leading off along a small footpath to the right, which descends through the trees to join a track. Turn left, then take a footpath to the right. At a fork take the left-hand path, following the waymarks to veer to the left downhill. ◄ Turn right down a track to a junction at the edge of **Windstein**. The GR53 goes right, downhill, passing the path to **Vieux Windstein Castle** on the left, to reach the former Auberge Aux Deux Châteaux (now chambres d'hôtes). The Hôtel du Windstein is about 1km off-route down the road from here.

The scattered houses of Windstein appear through the trees ahead.

Windstein to Grand Wintersberg, 7.5km (4.5 miles), 2hr 45min

The route crosses directly in front of the auberge, passing between the buildings and leaving by a track up into woods. Take a path to the right, going uphill to **Nouveau Windstein Castle**. Follow the sign to Niederbronn, passing around the ruins, then turn right on meeting a track, which leads down to a minor road. Turn right. The road soon becomes a forest track. Leave by a footpath down to the left and very soon, take another path left. Continue downhill to the road at Vallon de Gruenenthal.

Cross over and go up the track opposite. About 5min later take a footpath down to the left then continue along the slope above a road for perhaps a kilometre, finally dropping down to join the road just outside Wineckerthal. Turn right into the village then leave by a minor road to the left, following this over a stream. Beyond the bridge turn right onto a footpath signed to Grand Wintersberg.

Cross an entrance track, then take a footpath uphill to the left, to a road. Follow the Route Forestière du Buchwald, opposite, to the house at Buchwald, then turn half right towards Col de Borneberg. Join a track and carry straight on but very soon leave to the left.

Look out for a footpath climbing steeply to the left, crossing two forest tracks. Where the path emerges onto a third, look to the right for the footpath continuing up the hill, and on meeting a larger track, go right.

The GR53 crosses a junction and meanders among beech trees, clearly waymarked, to reach a track. Turn left to Col de Borneberg and continue to the small shelter at Col du Pottaschkopf.

Landscape of the Northern Vosges

From this tower there is a fine view as far as the Black Forest.

Just behind the shelter, take a footpath leading to Col de la Liese about 0.5km further on (the Club Vosgien chalet serves drinks on Sundays and holidays). Cross the road opposite the chalet and take a footpath, hairpinning upwards to the late19th-century outlook tower on **Grand Wintersberg** (580m). ◄

Grand Wintersberg to Niederbronn-les-Bains, 4km (2.5 miles), 1hr 25min

Hotels, campsite, restaurants, cafés and shops in Niederbronn.

Follow the path signposted 'Source Lichteneck' and cross the next track (blue circle route). Very soon after, a sign directs the GR53 down a path to the left. (Do not continue straight on to Niederbronn by Camp Celtique.)

Hairpin down, cross two tracks and turn right down a third, then soon leave by a footpath to the right. Descend some steps and turn left for a short distance before taking a path to the right. Turn left and continue down this wooded valley.

On meeting a track, go downhill to a busy road. Turn left and pass the buildings of Source Celtique (the waters from this ancient spring are bottled, and widely available). The route soon leaves by a path up into woods on the left and reaches a road.

Turn right, downhill, towards the centre of **Niederbronn-les-Bains** (the uphill fork leads to the campsite, about 1km away). Turn right at the Passage Publique du Parc Grunelius, and where the tarmac ends fork left down to a street, then turn left to reach the centre of this lively little spa town.

ALSATIAN LANGUAGE

In the streets and shops of Niederbronn-les-Bains local people can sometimes be heard chatting in the local Alsatian language. This is widely used, especially in the north of Alsace, particularly by older people. It went into decline in the years after World War II, but more recently has been recognised as making a valuable contribution to local heritage.

SECTION 2
GR53 NIEDERBRONN-LES-BAINS TO SAVERNE

Niederbronn-les-Bains

Most of this section of the walk is through forest in the heartland of the Northern Vosges regional park. Although not high, the landscape is far from flat, with the route leading over a succession of small hills and valleys, and only at occasional lookout points can the extent of the forest really be appreciated. In these quiet woods it is possible that the walker will glimpse wild boar or marten.

Niederbronn-les-Bains is a spa town with ample facilities and many walking trails close by. The archaeological centre for the Northern Vosges is also located here. Just outside the town the GR53 passes the ruins of Wasenbourg Castle, the first of several castles in this section. Grand Arnsbourg Castle stands above the path on an elevated rocky outcrop and the considerable ruins of Lichtenberg Castle, set within a huge defensive wall, dominate the village below.

Lichtenberg is one of several villages passed en route, each with its own character. La Petite-Pierre sits on a fortified promontory, and although small has many tourist facilities. The headquarters of the regional park are situated in the buildings of the restored castle.

In Graufthal some unusual rock dwellings, *maisons troglodytiques*, lie close to the route. These cottages, built into the sandstone cliff, were inhabited until

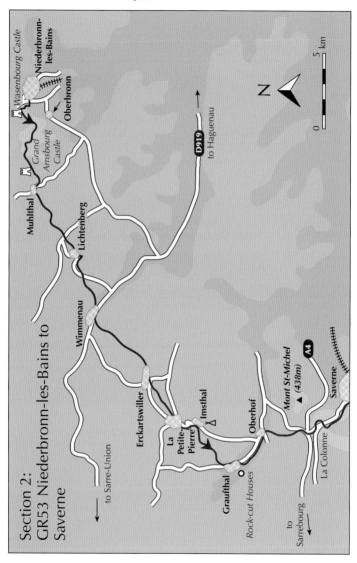

Section 2:
GR53 Niederbronn-les-Bains to Saverne

Wasenbourg Castle

the 1950s. Further on, the route skirts a series of crags, including a particularly impressive overhang known as the Saut du Prince Charles.

This section can be comfortably walked in three days, with suggested stops at Lichtenberg and La Petite-Pierre. A single stop at Wimmenau would allow you to complete the section in two days, but be prepared for a long second day.

SECTION SUMMARY TABLE			
Start	**Distance**	**Ascent/Descent**	**Time**
Niederbronn-les-Bains	3km (2 miles)	250m/0m	1hr 15min
Wasenbourg Castle	8km (5 miles)	100m/330m	2hr 30min
Muhlthal	7.5km (4.5 miles)	300m/200m	2hr 15min
Lichtenberg	6km (3.5 miles)	0m/100m	1hr 45min
Wimmenau	6.5km (4 miles)	100m/80m	2hr
Erckartswiller	4km (2.5 miles)	160m/40m	1hr 15min
La Petite-Pierre	7km (4.5 miles)	140m/280m	2hr 15min
Graufthal	12km (7.5 miles)	200m/210m	3hr 45min

SECTION 2
Niederbronn-les-Bains to Saverne

Start	Niederbronn-les-Bains
Distance	54km (33.5 miles)
Maps	IGN TOP100 sheet 112; TOP75 sheet 027; Club Vosgien 1:50,000 sheets 1/8 and part of 2/8

Niederbronn-les-Bains to Wasenbourg Castle, 3km (2 miles), 1hr 15min
Hotels, campsite, restaurants, cafés and shops in Niederbronn.

Cross the bridge opposite the tourist office, then turn right to walk alongside the stream through the park. After the amenities block turn left to join the road, then right and soon left, under the railway bridge. Take the Allée des Tilleuls on the right.

After about 1km pass under a road bridge, then turn sharply left. This leads onto a track that soon runs parallel to a busy road. After a very short distance turn right at a waymark and follow the path which zigzags uphill to a vehicle track. A sign indicates a turn to the right, not along the track, but onto a footpath on the far side that heads off through the forest.

After about 20min the path emerges onto another track, close to the remains of a charcoalburners' site. Go to the right for a short distance and look out for a path branching off left. Follow this up to a junction by **Wasenbourg Castle**, which is worth a short detour off-route.

Wasenbourg Castle to Muhlthal, 8km (5 miles), 2hr 30min
Restaurant (high class) in Muhlthal.

Retrace your steps to the junction, then follow the path, signposted to Kreuztannen, which soon reaches Cabane

Kohlhutte. Take the broad gravel track to the right, and fork left further uphill to the clearing at Kreuztannen. Carry on straight across, but just a few hundred metres beyond, watch out for waymarks to a footpath on the right. The route winds up to reach the lookout tower at Wasenkoepfel.

Follow the main path beyond the tower, through woods and along the edge of a grassy clearing. This soon reaches a major junction where the GR53 heads left to Col de l'Ungerthal, where there is a small shelter. Leave the col by the path just to the left of the shelter, signposted to Holdereck, leading to the road at Col du Holdereck. On the far side, the GR53 takes the left-hand path towards Grand Arnsbourg.

Pass over the Grunschaft junction, and soon afterwards fork left, following a sunken gully as it descends to **Grand Arnsbourg Castle**. The ruins sit high on an exposed crag, but unfortunately, access is forbidden.

Pass to the right of the rock, cross two tracks, then emerge onto a third. Follow this to the left, downhill to the road, and turn right towards **Muhlthal**. Turn left where waymarked, just before a large restaurant.

Grand Arnsbourg Castle

Muhlthal to Lichtenberg,
7.5km (4.5 miles), 2hr 15min
Hotels/restaurants and gîte in Lichtenberg.

Cross the footbridge and follow the path to the right, close to the back of the restaurant, then cross another small bridge. The path rises and joins the end of a lane. Follow this to a T-junction and turn left, then soon left again onto a track by a lake.

The route takes a left fork signposted for Lichtenberg. Only a few minutes later turn right then immediately look out for a footpath to the left, which leads up through the forest for about half an hour. At Col du Baerenberg, turn right, but be prepared for the next junction which is easy to miss.

The church at Lichtenberg can soon be picked out on the hill ahead.

Within about 1km a signpost indicates that Niederbronn is 4hr 50min away. The GR leaves obliquely along a footpath to the left, but the path is currently not well waymarked. ◄ When the path meets a gravel track, take the left-hand, downhill direction, fork left 10min later, and on joining another track, keep straight on. At Pulverbruecke a GR sign directs the route left onto a road.

Cross over, and take the waymarked footpath up through the woods, joining a wider track. The village of **Lichtenberg** is on the hill ahead, and the houses below form the hamlet of Picardie. The track climbs into woods and rises up behind Picardie, passes the end of a road, and curves downhill to a junction. Follow the sign left into Lichtenberg. There is a drinking water point outside the gîte.

Lichtenberg to Wimmenau, 6km (3.5 miles), 1hr 45min
Hotel/restaurant and shops in Wimmenau.

At a T-junction just beyond the village square, a short diversion to the left leads to Lichtenberg Castle. The GR53 turns right, then left along Rue du Vogelhardt. Continue as the path drops down fairly steeply and skirts a deep valley to emerge onto a country road. Turn right, but only briefly, then left at a sign to Wimmenau.

Forest track beyond Lichtenberg

The path crosses a vehicle track, then drops down to join a more major track on the right. Carry straight on, but look out for the next junction. Not far along the track the GR53 leaves to the right along a small footpath through open pine woodland. Follow this as it merges with another path and soon leads out onto a road. Turn left here, but after a few hundred metres a GR sign points along the first track to the right.

Turn left towards Wimmenau at a T-junction, then at the next junction carry on along the more minor track straight ahead. After a few minutes the route leaves by a well-signed path to the right.

45

Follow on through the forest for about half an hour, eventually reaching a substantial track where the GR route is directed left for just a few dozen metres before leaving to the right. The first houses of Wimmenau come into sight through the trees. The route crosses a road then continues along a footpath. Fork right to follow alongside the railway embankment.

The track leads into **Wimmenau**. Turn left and continue over the level crossing into the centre of the village, passing a baker's, then the village shop. On reaching the D157, cross over the River Moder to gain the D919.

Wimmenau to Erckartswiller, 6.5km (4 miles), 2hr

Turn right, then left up Rue Ritti, which becomes an earth track that heads towards the forest. At a junction with a choice of three ways, the GR takes the left-hand one, then a path to the right, to join another track.

From here to Erckartswiller, the route is easily followed through woodland, with the rocks at Ochsenstall providing added interest. Soon after entering the trees the GR53 forks right and keeps close to the forest edge. Within about 10min the route crosses a vehicle track and continues along a path to a junction where a waymark points left.

The GR forks left three times, before reaching a crossroads with the blue cross route (Ingwiller left, Wingensur-Moder right). Follow the prominent woodland path opposite. The route joins a more major track and continues to the rocks at Ochsenstall, where there are several overhangs and small caves. Just beyond, as the track curves away to the left, the GR leaves on a footpath to the right, signposted to La Petite-Pierre.

The path soon forks, the GR following the right-hand branch ahead. Some 5min later this joins a forest track on a bend and leads on past a junction into **Erckartswiller**.

Erckartswiller to La Petite-Pierre, 4km (2.5 miles), 1hr 15min

Hotels, gîte, restaurants, cafés and bakery in La Petite-Pierre.

Follow this lane through the village to meet the D813. The GR turns left, crosses a stream, then immediately turns right along a gravel track. This becomes a footpath which follows the edge of a field until a waymark diverts the route into woodland.

Within a few minutes, the footpath joins a more major path then crosses a track and takes a path diagonally to the right. This broad path is easily followed from here on, crossing one track and forking left at the next junction to lead up onto a short ridge with a deep, wooded valley first to one side, then to the other. After going through a cleft between two large rocks the path starts to descend, becoming a vehicle track which leads across an expanse of pastureland.

Turn left on the far side and go up to the road. Turn right, and continue downhill for about 1km to a T-junction in the centre of **La Petite-Pierre**. The village currently has no food shop, but a right turn leads past a *salon du thé*, which sells bread and some groceries.

La Petite-Pierre to Graufthal,
7km (4.5 miles), 2hr 15min
Campsite and hotel/restaurant in Imsthal;
hotel and restaurants in Graufthal.

Turn left along Rue Principale, which is flanked by hotels and restaurants. Take the minor road to the right, signed to the Maison du Parc and tourist office. Follow this past the war memorial, then leave to the left, opposite the tourist office, by a narrow road alongside old fortifications. This little road runs through a rocky gap, then along a very short elevated ridge before passing the Poet's Garden, which provides a good lookout point over the fortified village and castle.

The GR forks right twice, and soon leads off to the right to the Rocher du Corbeau, an elevated bluff that provides an excellent viewing platform over the wooded surroundings.

Coming down from the promontory the route takes a little footpath, and soon passes below a second rock. The path hairpins down to the left, zigzags downhill, crosses three tracks, and reaches the road down in the valley. Turn right, passing the **Imsthal campsite** and signs for an auberge, until a lake comes into view on the right of the road. The GR takes a little lane which branches to the right, skirts the lake and heads across the valley.

When the lane goes off left towards houses, the GR is signposted to the right along a track, but almost immediately leaves on a footpath to the left. This little path gains height through beech woods, crossing vehicle tracks on the way up. Follow this for about 1.5km to a road near the brow of the hill. Cross over, and take the path that twists to the left and soon runs parallel to the road.

Within about 10min the path winds down to a vehicle track close to a sports field. Cross the track and continue on the far side. The path soon merges with another vehicle track, which the GR route leaves to the right, only 50 metres further along. Follow this little path for almost 1km down the hill to reach a road by some fishponds. Turn left into the village of **Graufthal**.

A diversion to the right reaches the line of rock-cut houses partly built into the cliff face.

Graufthal

48

ROCK-CUT HOUSES

The 70m-high sandstone cliff behind the little village of Graufthal shelters some of the last remaining rock-cut houses in the region. In the Middle Ages several small caves in the rock face were used by the nearby abbey as storerooms for provisions and firewood, and over the years some of these shelters were converted into dwellings. The earliest date of occupation is unclear, but one cottage has a lintel dated 1760, and the last occupant lived here right up until 1958. These primitive cave houses provided the most basic of accommodation, and now form a small museum.

Graufthal to Saverne, 12km (7.5 miles), 3hr 45min
Bar/restaurant in Oberhof; hotels, youth hostel, campsite, restaurants, cafés and shops in Saverne.

On reaching a more major road on a bend, continue straight on to leave the village, and after a few hundred metres turn right beside the cemetery. ▸

The road soon crosses a stream, and the GR53 leaves to the left. Follow this track for the next 3km, staying in the bottom of the valley, roughly parallel with the little stream. The track reaches a road where the route turns left, crossing a bridge and continuing until directed right along a vehicle track. From here a short diversion along the road reaches the inn at **Oberhof**.

After a few hundred metres there is a junction where several paths meet. Turn right, signposted for Saverne, following a path which crosses two tracks, then finally joins with a third. This soon meets a vehicle track, and the route carries on in much the same direction.

Turn left on reaching a lane, which comes out onto a road, where the signpost may be hidden in foliage. Turn right and follow the road for over 1km, crossing a bridge over the railway then a motorway, to reach **La Colonne**, where a sandstone pillar stands in front of the Saverne–Phalsbourg road.

The GR leaves by a small footpath to the left, then turns right towards Kaltwiller, and soon leads to a major track junction called MF Kaltwiller.

From the road you can see the headstone of Catherine Ottermann, nicknamed Felsekäth (Cliff Kate), the last inhabitant of the rock-cut houses, who died in 1958.

Turn right and cross the main road, onto the lane opposite, then turn left along a little path that heads through woodland and emerges onto another lane. Turn right, but only briefly, before leaving to the left beside a picnic bench, along the indicated footpath.

This path crosses a section of the **Fossé des Pandours**, two large banks separated by a ditch. These substantial defences have been dated to pre-Roman times and were probably built by Celtic people. The name derives from the 18th century, when the Pandours, mercenaries fighting for the Duke of Lorraine, used the ditch as a line of defence.

Keep straight on to Usspann, and leave by the footpath opposite, keeping to the main path until, some minutes later, the route crosses a lane, and drops down the side of a steep valley. A large sandstone outcrop appears on the left, the first of several. The site known as Saut du Prince Charles is a particularly impressive overhang a little further on. This now quiet place was once a major thoroughfare, as evidenced by the deep wheel ruts worn into the rock.

Follow the main path down to a turning area; the GR veers left, emerges onto a road, and continues to a T-junction. Turn left, passing factory premises, to meet the N4. Turn right, cross the railway bridge, and take the first road to the left. Turn half right at a traffic island and go up Grand'Rue, a busy street lined with shops, to reach the canal and the centre of **Saverne**.

SAVERNE

A Saverne townhouse

While villages throughout Alsace contain many traditional half-timbered buildings, Saverne contains examples of more prosperous townhouses. Roofs are sharply pointed, sometimes with ornamented gables and rows of dormer windows. The house facades, often brightly coloured, can expose plain wooden beams or incorporate more richly decorated woodwork, testifying to the skill of local craftsmen. The more opulent houses often have overhanging projections, oriel windows or balconies extending out into the streets. The Maison Katz on Grand'Rue is a particularly fine example, where even the beams high above the street are covered in carved decoration.

Saverne's key position, where the Zorn Valley cuts through the Vosges, made it a prosperous trading centre from Roman times. The valley was later used for the route of the Marne–Rhine Canal, which now provides a colourful marina in the centre of the town. The many fine buildings include the Château des Rohan, the early 17th-century house of Maison Katz and the old castle.

Saverne is proud of the many contrasting gardens found in the locality. A rosary contains over 7000 rose bushes, the château is set in a park that overlooks the canal marina, and there is a botanic garden to the north-west of the town.

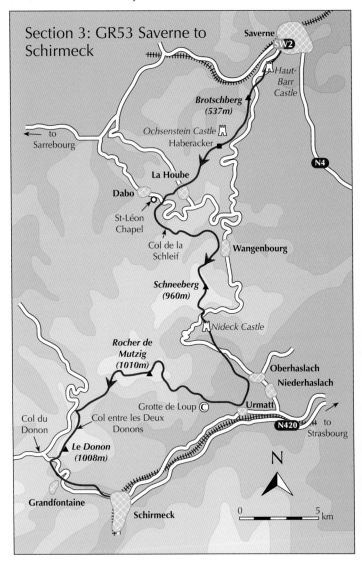

Section 3: GR53 Saverne to Schirmeck

Saverne

SW2

Haut-
Barr
Castle

*Brotschberg
(537m)*

Ochsenstein Castle
Haberacker

← to
Sarrebourg

N4

La Hoube

Dabo

St-Léon
Chapel

Col de la
Schleif

Wangenbourg

*Schneeberg
(960m)*

Nideck Castle

*Rocher de
Mutzig
(1010m)*

Oberhaslach
Niederhaslach

Grotte de Loup ℂ

Urmatt

Col du
Donon

Col entre les Deux
Donons

N420 → to
Strasbourg

▲ *Le Donon
(1008m)*

N

0   5 km

Grandfontaine

Schirmeck

SECTION 3
GR53 SAVERNE TO SCHIRMECK

The wooded hills of the Northern Vosges

This section starts in the historic town of Saverne, lying in a valley that has long been a gateway between France and the rest of Europe.

Most of the walking is across wooded hills, but compared with the sections to the north, this part of the route involves a little more climbing. The path crosses lower hills then rises up to the summit of Schneeberg at 960m. It then drops to the valley of the Bruche before climbing again to cross Le Donon where it meets the GR5. The end of this section, the small town of Schirmeck, is once again down in the valley of the Bruche.

Some striking sandstone features are encountered along the way, such as Haut-Barr Castle, sitting on two close crags connected by a bridge. Further south the Rocher de Dabo, a huge, steep-sided rock topped by the St-Léon Chapel, creates a remarkable silhouette. Beyond Urmatt the isolated sandstone arch of La Porte de Pierre is another scenic highlight.

Many good viewpoints are passed along the way. At Nideck, the lower of the two castles stands guard at the top of a cliff, dominating the wooded gorge below, while a nearby stream cascades down the head of this narrow valley, forming an impressive waterfall. There are also good all-round views from the summit of Le Donon (1008m).

This section can be walked in three days, with suggested stops at Wangenbourg and Urmatt. The third day is strenuous, however, as it is long and includes steep climbs, so you might consider a further stop at a hotel at Col du Donon, otherwise accommodation on this final stretch is limited. Be aware that there is currently no accommodation in the town of Schirmeck itself, although there are possibilities in neighbouring villages.

SECTION SUMMARY TABLE			
Start	Distance	Ascent/Descent	Time
Saverne	3km (2 miles)	270m/0m	1hr
Haut-Barr Castle	7km (4.5 miles)	100m/80m	2hr 25min
Haberacker	6.5km (4 miles)	180m/120m	2hr 10min
Dabo Road Junction	7.5km (4.5 miles)	210m/250m	2hr 15min
Wangenbourg	8km (5 miles)	460m/420m	2hr 45min
Nideck Castle	5km (3 miles)	0m/240m	1hr 30min
Oberhaslach	3.5km (2 miles)	20m/60m	1hr 10min
Urmatt	10.5km (6.5 miles)	750m/0m	3hr 45min
Rocher de Mutzig	12km (7.5 miles)	270m/550m	3hr 45min
Col du Donon	7.5km (4.5 miles)	0m/410m	2hr 15min

Looking towards Le Donon

SECTION 3
Saverne to Schirmeck

Start	Saverne
Distance	70.5km (44 miles)
Maps	IGN TOP100 sheet 112; TOP75 sheet 027; Club Vosgien 1:50,000 sheets 1/8 and 4/8

Saverne to Haut-Barr Castle, 3km (2 miles), 1hr
Hotels, youth hostel, campsite, restaurants, cafés and shops in Saverne; café/restaurant in Haut-Barr.

From the canal bridge in Grand'Rue, take the towpath west. After only a few minutes, leave by a path to climb some steps to a road. Turn left, then very soon right along Rue Dell. Cross over the first junction, then turn right along Rue Général Leclerc and continue for about a kilometre, passing a sign to the campsite. The route diverts left at Rue Parc Celtique, then soon right to reach a signboard at Bildstoeckel de la Trinité.

Follow the GR53 up a footpath through the trees. After about 10min fork left, and soon after some benches and a display board take the path indicated to the right. In about 5min look out for a small path leaving at a tight angle to the left. Continue upwards to **Haut-Barr Castle**. ▸

The castle and chapel are accessible to visitors and there are sweeping views from the highest level.

Haut-Barr Castle to Haberacker, 7km (4.5 miles), 2hr 25min

Leave the car park, passing the Chappe Telegraph Tower, and continue parallel to the road. Just before Grand Geroldseck Castle the GR53 forks left to follow around the base of the mound, where a short diversion reaches these extensive ruins. A little further on, the path to Petit Geroldseck Castle leaves to the left, and again the GR53 continues round the base. Petit Geroldseck has little more than the stump of the tower remaining.

The route meets a road at Table des Sorcières, and continues along the track opposite. Very soon take a path left, following waymarks which lead up to the summit of **Brotschberg** (537m), where there is a small shelter and a lookout tower rising well above the treetops. The GR53 leaves to the left by a path to the Rocher and Grotte du Brotsch.

The route goes downhill through spruce woods, forks left at a junction and merges with a track to continue to Rocher du Brotsch, a shapely outcrop of sandstone that makes a fine lookout point. The GR53 is the first path to

The bridge at Haut-Barr Castle

the left when descending from the rock (avoid the second path, to Grand Krappenfels). The route hairpins round to pass beneath the overhang, where there is a large cave, the Grotte du Brotsch. After a few more hairpins the path reaches a track. Follow this to the right to a junction and turn left, then at a large stone cistern turn left again and take the route downhill to join a road at a small car park.

Rocher du Brotsch

Turn right, and follow around a bend past the Maison Forestière Schaeferplatz to reach a picnic place. Just beyond, a sign to **Haberacker** points to the right along a forest footpath. Go left at the next fork and follow along the side of a slope, parallel to the road, to a sign at Lothringer-Baechel.

Almost opposite, the route continues to Carrefour du Billebaum. Turn right along the road towards a huge preserved beech stump. Just before this, leave to the left onto a footpath, again signposted to Haberacker. ▶ Turn left onto a road just by Carrefour du Haberacker and fork left uphill.

Across the valley, rock outcrops on the skyline are topped by the ruins of Ochsenstein Castle.

Haberacker to Dabo Road Junction, 6.5km (4 miles), 2hr 10min

Hotel/restaurant in La Hoube (0.5km off-route); gîte and campsite in Dabo; restaurant, cafés and shop in Dabo village (1.5km off-route).

57

Keep on the road for about 5min, then turn left along a path into the forest, signposted to Geissfelswasen. On reaching a wide track the route initially runs alongside, then drops onto it. After only a few hundred metres, fork right, and leave again to the left by a path up the banking.

Turn right at a substantial path, then on meeting a track at a bend the route carries on ahead to reach the crossroads at La Hardt. Just before this, a gap in the trees allows a glimpse of Dabo rock, about 3km distant. Turn right towards La Hoube, but just as the track curves right, leave it by a path that goes straight ahead into the trees. In a few minutes this crosses a small track, then turns left to run downhill beside it.

Cross the stream at the bottom of the valley and turn right, up the wooded bank, then left up a stony footpath. This rises quite steeply between two tumbledown walls towards **La Hoube**. Go up a grassy path that emerges onto the road downhill from the church, (the Hôtel des Vosges is about 500m away, along the right fork at the church).

Turn right, downhill, then go left along a grassy lane, pass along the top of a low, broad wall, cross a road and enter forest.

Go across a small track and carry on for about 10min, curving round the end of a valley and rising through mature woodland. On meeting a major track, go downhill to a junction. Cross the footbridge almost opposite and climb the far bank, initially by stone steps, to meet a road. Turn right, uphill, and follow around a bend. At a T-junction, the GR53 turns left along a quiet road to reach the D45. **Dabo** is about 1km off-route from here.

Dabo Road Junction to Wangenbourg, 7.5km (4.5 miles), 2hr 15min

Shelter at Col de la Schleif; gîte in Engenthal (1km off-route); hotels, campsite, restaurants and bakery/café in Wangenbourg.

Two roads leave on the far side of the D45. To visit the Rocher de Dabo, divert to the right, but the GR53 takes the Route Forestière du Chat Noir to the left, passing Dabo campsite and gîte. Take a footpath, running parallel to the road and a little below it.

> The intriguing **Rocher de Dabo** draws the eye from whichever direction it is approached. This strange and imposing flat-topped rock is yet another example of the effects of sandstone weathering – little wonder that such a site has been fortified for centuries. There was a castle here since at least the 12th century. Invading French forces seized the site in 1677, and two years later, blew up the castle. Nothing can now be seen of the defences.
>
> Stones from the ruins were used to build the current chapel, which dates from 1890. The St-Léon Chapel is dedicated to Léon IX, pope from 1048 to 1054. Léon belonged to a powerful family of local landowners, and is the only pope to have come from Alsace.

After a few minutes the route briefly rejoins the road, providing good views of the chapel and rock, before

St-Léon Chapel, Dabo

The path passes Le Rutschfelsen, a stone with curious depressions on its surface. ◄

leaving to the left. Cross a major track and continue through woodland. At a T-junction turn left towards Col de la Schleif, and climb steadily through thick conifer woods. ◄

On emerging onto a road turn right, then soon leave to the left at **Col de la Schleif**, where there is a shelter. Leave by the track opposite, heading downhill. The next turn is easy to miss. The track descends for about 0.5km, then takes a slight bend to the right followed by a sharp bend to the left. In between, look for a small footpath dropping very steeply to the left by rocky steps, down to a tiny stream. The arrow and a waymark indicating this path are not obvious.

The path follows the stream down the valley and crosses a bridge. Turn right, and after a couple of minutes take a footpath to the left. When this meets a road, cross over, and follow the waymarks by the side of the former Auberge Rosskopf to cross a small concrete bridge. To reach the gîte Grand Tétras, leave the route and continue down the road. Climb the bank beyond and follow the path, turn left along a broad track for a few hundred metres, then leave by a footpath to the right.

Pass the Fontaine Helwig, cross a track, then at the next track go left for a few minutes, then right and continue along the hillside with a view of Wangenbourg and its castle and church. ◄ To visit **Wangenbourg**, leave the GR just beyond the water tank, and go down the steps at Impasse de l'Escalier.

The grassy top of a water tank forms a good lookout point. ◄

Wangenbourg to Nideck Castle, 8km (5 miles), 2hr 45min
Shelter at Schneeberg (0.5km off-route).

The route now climbs steadily for about 1hr 45min to the summit of Schneeberg at 960m. Continue uphill and keep to the right-hand branch where the GR531 branches left. At an oblique junction turn left along a track that now levels out. Turn off right after a few minutes on a path that rises steadily along the side of the hill and eventually joins a vehicle track.

Take this to the left and at the next junction, turn sharply right uphill, then sharply left just afterwards. At the Col du Schneeberg leave by the path opposite to join a track going left, then after about 15min a detour to the right leads up to the summit of **Schneeberg**, a deeply cut block of rock with a *table d'orientation* (outlook indicator).

On leaving the rock, retrace your steps to the first junction where there is a sign to a shelter just off-route, then follow a path through conifer forest. At a vehicle track, turn right, then left, following a GR sign pointing downhill, with a deep, wooded valley to the left. This rocky footpath eventually leads down a short metal ladder to a track. Continue downhill and at the next track cross straight over to descend through the forest.

On meeting a road turn right for about 0.4km, then just around a bend to the right watch out for waymarks to the left and go down past the first, smaller **castle at Nideck** to the second, not far below.

Nideck Castle to Oberhaslach,
5km (3 miles), 1hr 30min
Café/gîte at Nideck, gîte and campsite at Luttenbach; hotel/restaurants and shops in Oberhaslach (1km off-route).

Take a footpath dropping to the right of the castle. This leads down the side of a deep valley and crosses a small stream to reach a lookout point over the Hasel Valley, a wooded gorge with cliffs on both sides. ▶ The original route continues down the steep, rocky path to reach the Cascade du Nideck, where a stream plunges down the cliff face, a spectacular sight after heavy rain. Follow the footpath down the valley – the clifftop position of the castle becomes more impressive from further down the path.

The path emerges onto a road by a café/gîte. Turn left, then soon right to cross two little bridges. The path runs alongside the stream and soon reaches a junction. Bear right, signposted to Urmatt, and continue along the woodland path, passing a spur to the campsite and gîte of Luttenbach.

At the time of writing, the route here was diverted temporarily due to a rockfall.

When the path comes near the road, turn right, taking a footpath that winds its way through woodland, and comes out on a gravel track where the route goes left, then immediately right to continue along the hillside.

The GR53 enters **Oberhaslach** by Rue de la Forêt, then turns left down a road towards a pond.

Oberhaslach to Urmatt, 3.5km (2 miles), 1hr 10min
Hotels, restaurants and shops in Urmatt.

The facilities of the village lie straight ahead, 1km off-route. Just before the pond turn sharply into Rue du Mittenbach, then left into Rue du Grempil to climb steeply. At the end of the road turn left and follow the main track. For the next two kilometres, follow the waymarks carefully on various tracks through the forest.

Join a track and follow it to the left for about 10min, then on meeting another track again bear left to continue in much the same direction. Keep on the track as it curves right, then turns right. At a T-junction, turn left, then very soon fork left.

At the edge of **Urmatt** take the road to the right (Rue de la Forêt), and follow it downhill to Rue de Molsheim. (A left turn here reaches the centre of the village.)

Urmatt to Rocher de Mutzig, 10.5km (6.5 miles), 3hr 45min

Turn right up Rue de Molsheim, and fork right by a *fontaine* with drinking water. Continue up the road, ignoring an ambiguous arrow to the left. Where the road curves left, leave by a footpath to the right, beside another fontaine.

At a junction, turn right and continue onto the Route Forestière du Kappelbronn. After about a kilometre, watch out for a rough track joining from the left, and take the footpath obliquely left here to cross one track and join another.

Go over a crossroads, towards Kappelbronn. The track climbs beside a stream, passing Route Forestière de la Grotte du Loup as the valley begins to narrow. The

cave of **Grotte du Loup** appears on the opposite side of the stream.

Rocher de Mutzig

Fork left on Route Forestière de la Turbine, pass a small shed, and follow the curve to the left, ignoring a grassy track ahead. At the next sharp bend to the left, take a footpath straight on, uphill, which emerges onto a major track. Turn left for a short distance then turn right by an upright stone where a sign directs towards Rocher de Mutzig.

By a wooden building, take the track going uphill, then leave by a path to the right, zigzagging upwards. A few minutes later, a sign to Porte de Pierre indicates a hairpin to the right.

At a forest track look right for a path up the bank opposite, to continue zigzagging uphill. After about 10min watch out for another point where there is a footpath straight ahead, but the route continues upwards as indicated by a waymark and cairn. Cross a forest track onto a footpath almost opposite, then at the next track avoid the false trail which scrambles up the bank on the far side. Turn right, along the track to an obvious junction, then turn sharply left and immediately right on a path which climbs to the splendid rock outcrop of Porte de Pierre.

Turn left back into the woods, then fork left uphill and climb steadily, curving round the side of the valley. Turn left on meeting a broader track to reach the **Rocher de Mutzig** (1010m).

Rocher de Mutzig to Col du Donon, 12km (7.5 miles), 3hr 45min
Hotels and restaurants at Col du Donon.

> This track is known as Le Balcon and gives a broad view, with the two summits in the distance of Le Donon and its smaller neighbour, Le Petit Donon.

The GR53 is signposted to the right to Le Donon, just before the outlook rock. The path curves round below the face of the rock and hairpins down. Follow this to the shelter at Col du Narion, and go over the crossroads. On reaching a forest track, turn left, avoiding the footpath opposite. ◄

After about 35min the track hairpins sharply left. A lesser track leaves the end of the hairpin, going uphill, but look carefully for a footpath to the left of this, going downhill and signposted to Baraque Carrée. On reaching a broad track, turn right, but look out for a path to the left, which is quite steep and rocky at the top. Descend to the shelter at La Baraque Carrée.

Leave by Route Forestière de la Corrière, contouring around the slope for about half an hour, then rising towards the ridge. On meeting another track turn right to Col de la Côte de l'Engin. This marks the end of the GR53; the GR5 continues to the south.

> Just beside the route is a World War I bunker. It is thought provoking to spend a few minutes investigating these underground chambers, although you will need your torch.

The GR5 long distance route starts on the Dutch coast and comes down through the plains of Lorraine to join the end of the GR53 at the Col de la Côte de l'Engin. South from here, as far as Ballon d'Alsace, the GR5 route still uses red rectangles as waymarks. ◄

Turn left just before the road and continue for over 1km. The mock Greco-Roman temple on Le Donon comes into view ahead. Fork right to **Col entre les Deux Donons**, then turn right past a shelter and replica marker stone, and fork right uphill.

A few minutes later, turn sharply left onto a track and follow it uphill, then soon leave by a footpath to the right, hairpinning up to meet a broad track. Turn right, then take a footpath up to the left. This zigzag path climbs to the summit of **Le Donon**, passing a small World War I shelter on the way. A waymark indicates the route up from the shelter.

The most obvious ruin to be seen on the summit of **Le Donon** today is a Greco-Roman style temple, but this only dates from 1869. Various Celtic and Gallic gods were worshipped here, but most of the remains are from the Roman period. The Roman temple complex appears to have been sacked in the fourth century, when the empire began to break down, but its final destruction came with the spread of Christianity in the seventh and eighth centuries. Several archaeological digs have produced a wealth of evidence, and some modern reconstructions mark these sites. One stone to look out for is just beyond the temple – it shows a bas-relief of a lion and wild boar in confrontation.

The temple at Le Donon

On the summit of Le Donon go to the left of the temple down some steps, following under the overhanging rock with replica carvings. Turn left at a more obvious path and wend your way down between remains and interpretation boards. Take a broad footpath to the left of an aerial downhill, to descend steps and cross a road on two occasions.

On reaching the D392, the GR5 goes left, but the hotels at Col du Donon are uphill to the right.

Col du Donon to Schirmeck,
7.5km (4.5 miles), 2hr 15min
Chambres d'hôtes in Wackenbach; restaurants, cafés and shops in Schirmeck; hotel and hostel in La Claquette (3km off-route).

Follow the road downhill, and just before it bends left, watch out for a footpath dropping to the right. Cross a vehicle track, and descend steadily through the woods, keeping on or close to a track for about two kilometres before waymarks lead off to the right to some steps down to a minor road. Cross the road and a footbridge to climb steeply to the D392.

Turn right, along the verge, for a short straight section – the houses of **Grandfontaine** are clustered in the valley ahead. Before the road bends left, take a footpath up the bank on the left. When this joins a track obliquely, carry straight on along the side of the valley, with the village of Wackenbach coming into view.

The path turns left up a side valley, forking right then swinging right, to cross a stream and climb to a road in Wackenbach. Go left, then up steps to the right to rejoin the road and turn right.

Take a road to the right as indicated and cross a turning circle onto Route Forestière de la Basse de la Scierie. Look out soon for a footpath to the left, leading down to a main road. Turn left to the edge of **Schirmeck**, and continue across the bridge into La Broque. Turn left by signs to a supermarket, skirt a parking area and cross the railway footbridge. Turn right down Avenue de la Gare towards Schirmeck town centre.

THE GR5
SCHIRMECK TO NYON

Lac des Perches (Section 7)

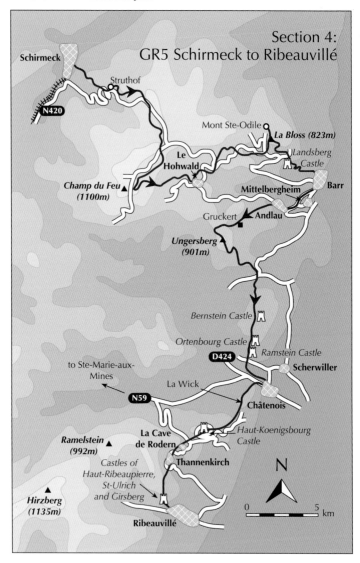

Section 4:
GR5 Schirmeck to Ribeauvillé

Schirmeck

N420

Struthof

Mont Ste-Odile

La Bloss (823m)

Landsberg Castle

Le Hohwald

Champ du Feu (1100m)

Mittelbergheim

Barr

Gruckert

Andlau

Ungersberg (901m)

Bernstein Castle

Ortenbourg Castle

D424

Ramstein Castle

Scherwiller

to Ste-Marie-aux-Mines

La Wick

N59

Châtenois

Ramelstein (992m)

La Cave de Rodern

Haut-Koenigsbourg Castle

Thannenkirch

Castles of Haut-Ribeaupierre, St-Ulrich and Girsberg

Hirzberg (1135m)

Ribeauvillé

N

0   5 km

SECTION 4
GR5 SCHIRMECK TO RIBEAUVILLÉ

Schirmeck

This section visits both elevated viewpoints in the hills and old Alsatian towns on the edge of the plain, passing a scattering of historic places on the way. The convent of Mont Ste-Odile is set on a rocky promontory, with the enigmatic remains of the Mur Païen, a massive ancient wall, surrounding the hill. A number of castles in varying stages of ruin and reconstruction lie on the route, foremost among them being Haut-Koenigsbourg, which can be seen from many miles away. The fortified church at Châtenois is another reminder of unsettled times. An unhappy period of more recent history is remembered at the concentration camp of Struthof, now partly preserved as a museum.

While the first part of this section is through forested hills, at Barr the route drops down to the foothills, where vineyards have long been a mainstay of the local way of life. The wealth generated from wine production is reflected in the prosperity of the several small towns and villages, with their many traditional houses. The final part of the section passes a sequence of three ruined castles as it drops down into Ribeauvillé, a lively town with a maze of narrow backstreets.

The walk involves a number of climbs and descents, but the steep stretches do not extend for very long. It is possible to complete this section in four days, with suggested stops at La Serva, Barr and Châtenois. The stretch from Barr to Châtenois is long, and a further stop at Andlau is a possibility.

On the road to Andlau

SECTION SUMMARY TABLE

Start	Distance	Ascent/Descent	Time
Schirmeck	5km (3 miles)	380m/0m	1hr 30min
Struthof	10.5km (6.5 miles)	380m/0m	3hr 15min
Col du Champ du Feu	6.5km (4 miles)	0m/510m	2hr
Le Hohwald	9.5km (6 miles)	290m/100m	3hr
Mont Ste-Odile	8km (5 miles)	70m/630m	2hr 30min
Barr	3.5km (2.5 miles)	40m/20m	1hr 15min
Andlau	7.5km (4.5 miles)	680m/0m	2hr 45min
Ungersberg	8.5km (5.5 miles)	180m/540m	3hr
Bernstein Castle	8.5km (5.5 miles)	0m/350m	2hr 30min
Châtenois	5km (3 miles)	210m/0m	1hr 30min
La Wick	4km (2.5 miles)	330m/0m	1hr 30min
Haut-Koenigsbourg	4km (2.5 miles)	0m/250m	1hr 15min
Thannenkirch	6km (3.5 miles)	170m/410m	2hr

SECTION 4
Schirmeck to Ribeauvillé

Start	Schirmeck
Distance	86.5km (54 miles)
Maps	IGN TOP100 sheet 122; TOP75 sheets 027, 028; Club Vosgien 1:50,000 sheet 4/8

Schirmeck to Struthof, 5km (3 miles), 1hr 30min
Restaurants, cafés and shops in Schirmeck;
restaurant 0.5km before Struthof.

Cross the square beside the tourist office and continue across a parking area. Climb the steps then follow the path to the castle, which is actually a recent reconstruction. ▸

From the castle leave to the left along a broad track, passing a shelter, to reach a signposted junction. Take the path towards Struthof, follow this to some power-lines, then take the small footpath opposite heading into woods. This narrow path crosses two tracks and meets a third at a junction. Take the uphill track for a very short distance, and look out for a footpath peeling off to the left. This leads to a seat at a lookout point, then joins a vehicle track.

Turn left and follow this track for about a kilometre, curving around the head of the valley. Go past Route Forestière Roquel to the junction beyond, with a shelter just off-route. Take a small footpath to the left of Route Forestière du Struthof, which it joins after about 10min.

Turn left at a road, then at the restaurant Chez Dany, head up a steep stepped path almost opposite. This crosses the D130 on two occasions before reaching the entrance to **Struthof camp**.

Struthof concentration camp was sited here to provide a labour force to quarry the nearby pink granite, which had been identified as suitable for

It is worth glancing over the courtyard wall for a view over the town.

some of Hitler's grandiose architectural schemes. Initially, it was a forced labour camp, using deportees to work the quarries, but it soon became even grimmer, with medical experiments and extermination among its goals. About 40,000 people suffered here, 10,000 dying from overwork, disease, or execution.

Several of the camp buildings have been restored, and one of the blocks houses a small museum. A memorial to the many thousands who were deported stands by the cemetery.

Struthof to Col du Champ du Feu, 10.5km (6.5 miles), 3hr 15min
Hotel/restaurant in La Serva (1.5km off-route).

Turn left along the road, passing between the Struthof memorial and the wartime sand-extraction pit. Just beyond the camp, follow the signposted footpath down to the left, then turn right along a track leading back towards the road. On the far side is the Struthof quarry.

Turn left along a footpath just before the road, then left down a vehicle track. After about 5min watch out for a footpath to the right, indicated by a sign. This gains height through thick old forest, joins with a broader path, and emerges onto a road at Champ du Messin. A signpost points left towards **Champ du Feu** (1100m).

Follow alongside the road, with views of forested hills fading into the distance. Just beyond a stone shelter with a fontaine, the route goes left before curving back to cross the road. In about 15min, turn right along a footpath towards Champ du Feu.

At a junction with the road just to the left, turn right along a muddy track, and after about 1km turn right towards Rocher de Rathsamhausen. The path soon joins a track that emerges onto the road. Turn right. A signpost directs the route left along a path that merges with a track. Carry on to the left, downhill, and turn right towards the Ancienne Métairie.

Just before a log-sided shelter, the GR5 forks right towards Champ du Feu. This path crosses several junctions as it rises through beech woods and swings around the head of a valley. Cross a track and then fork right as waymarked to reach the edge of the woods at Col du Champ du Feu. For the auberge at La Serva, 1.5km off-route, take the footpath across the nature reserve opposite.

Col du Champ du Feu to Le Hohwald, 6.5km (4 miles), 2hr
Hotels/restaurants, gîte, campsite, cafés and shop in Le Hohwald.

Where the path emerges from the trees, turn sharply left to a fork where both paths head back into the woods. Take the left-hand path towards Le Hohwald, continue downhill to a broad track, and turn left. A few minutes later turn right towards the Source de l'Andlau, a small spring trickling by the pathside. The path drops through woods for the next 2km, crossing several tracks and roads to reach the Cascade d'Andlau. ▶

Staying on the GR misses the best views of the waterfall, so a short diversion down the red-spot path is recommended.

Cascade d'Andlau

73

Returning to the top of the falls, take the uphill fork as indicated. This crosses a second stream, then heads downhill to a road. Turn right, but then take a path along the bank to the left. This leads through woodland to the perimeter of a campsite. Just by the site entrance, take the road ahead into **Le Hohwald**. Turn left at a more major road.

Le Hohwald to Mont Ste-Odile, 9.5km (6 miles), 3hr
Hotel and café/restaurant at Mont Ste-Odile.

Turn left along Rue Ste-Odile, and opposite the *salle polyvalente* (community building), which functions as a gîte d'étape, take a footpath on the far side of the car park. The GR5 forks right where the Grande Ceinture path (blue discs) forks left.

Fork right again in about 15min, and continue downhill to a road, taking the path opposite towards Welschbruch. Fork left, uphill, just beyond a small stream, then 5min later take a footpath to the left. After a stretch between two banks, join a track running alongside. Turn right at a road, then take the D130 left. Just up the road, take a footpath to the right, passing the back of the auberge at Welschbruch (currently closed). At a junction, take the downhill path towards Breitmatt.

The route crosses the yellow cross route and reaches Carrefour de la Breitmatt after almost half an hour. Cross the road and follow signs to Ste-Odile. On joining a track at a hairpin, follow waymarks up to the left, and stay with this level track for about a kilometre to reach a bench at a viewpoint overlooking the hills towards Barr. Very soon, take the left-hand, higher path at a fork. This leads to Carrefour de la Bloss. The GR leaves between the D426 and D854, following the curve of the D426 to reach the substantial remains of the Mur Païen.

The massive 'pagan wall' of the **Mur Païen** is an intriguing feature. It is more than 10km long, 1.5m thick and 3m high at its best-preserved sections, but opinion among archaeologists is divided as to who built it, when and why. Some suggest that it was a defensive enclosure, others that it was a religious site. What is not in doubt is that it is an impressive piece of work, its huge sandstone blocks carefully fitted together.

Go through the gap in the wall, cross the yellow cross route, and after about 10min pass the Beckenfels, an outcrop of strangely shaped rocks. The GR5 now heads for Mont Ste-Odile, then returns to this point before continuing to Barr. Keep to the path to the left of the rocks, and take the footpath (marked piétons) from the car park to the convent on **Mont Ste-Odile**.

The legend of Saint Odile tells of her being born blind but miraculously regaining her sight. She founded a convent on the top of **Mont Ste-Odile** in about AD700, and pilgrims still come to the mountain to visit the saint's sarcophagus in the 12th-century chapel, and to seek healing for eye complaints at the sacred spring. There are fine views from the terrace surrounding the buildings.

Mont Ste-Odile convent

75

Mont Ste-Odile to Barr, 8km (5 miles), 2hr 30min
Hotels, campsite, restaurants, cafés and shops in Barr.

From the gateway of the convent head left down steps. A diversion reaches the sacred spring, but the GR5 turns right along the Chemin de la Croix. Retrace your steps to Beckenfels, and fork left for the onward route towards Barr.

After about 5min the path passes a shelter and lookout point. Turn left along a broader track, then cross over a junction to the summit of **La Bloss** (823m), and pass an open shelter before reaching the table d'orientation on Maennelstein.

Go left, downhill, at a fork, then turn left through the Mur Païen to Rocher du Wachtstein, where a natural pillar of rock has been joined to the old wall. The path down crosses one track and follows left on joining another, leading to Kiosque Jadelot, a shelter with a veranda suspended over an open view. Beyond the kiosque, fork left to drop steeply to a road at La Handschab. Cross over and carry on down, forking left.

Approaching Barr

The route passes close to the ruins of **Landsberg Castle**, off-route to the right beyond a large old house.

Stay with the main path, forking right, then turning sharply left at a hairpin. Keep following signs for Barr downhill to the right. The path continues along a bank and turns left just before reaching the shelter of Petit Kiosque. GR signs direct the route down to the right, passing Maison Forestière Moenkalb. Follow a lane for almost 1km, passing the first of many vineyards.

At a fork, leave by the path between the two roads, which crosses a lane twice before emerging onto a road. Take the path to the Hering monument, and leave to the right, with views over the town on the approach to **Barr**. Cross a road, then turn left down broad steps to carry on along Rue de l'Église.

Barr to Andlau, 3.5km (2.5 miles), 1hr 15min
Hotel and restaurants in Mittelbergheim (0.5km off-route); hotels, restaurants, cafés and shops in Andlau.

Go down Rue des Boulangers and continue along Rue Taufflieb and Rue Saint Marc. Cross the D854, taking the D362 towards Mittelbergheim. Just before reaching **Mittelbergheim** follow the waymarks along the road forking to the right. ▶ Cross the next junction onto a pleasant lane flanked by vineyards and at the D62, turn right into **Andlau**.

On the hillside above, two towers joined by a curtain wall form the distinctive ruins of Andlau Castle.

Andlau has a particularly fine **Romanesque church**, much of the building dating from the 12th century. There are some outstanding stone carvings on the west and north sides of the church, and also around the doorway, showing various Biblical scenes and mythical animals.

Andlau to Ungersberg, 7.5km (4.5 miles), 2hr 45min
Refuge at Gruckert.

Take the D425 through the centre of the village, past the church. When the major road bears right, carry on up

77

Rue Clemenceau, and at a fork take the road to the left climbing sharply. Continue through light woodland to reach another road, then turn left, uphill.

Where the track hairpins to the right, take the rough track ahead and climb to Col de Gruckert. The route goes behind the Amis de la Nature refuge at **Gruckert**, and continues across Carrefour du Hasselbach.

At Col de l'Ungersberg, take the track sharply left, signed to Ungersberg, the shapely wooded hill glimpsed through trees ahead. At a T-junction, turn left, going uphill more steeply, then continue upwards, following waymarks and signs along a hairpinning route to reach the lookout tower on the summit of **Ungersberg** (901m).

Ungersberg to Bernstein Castle, 8.5km (5.5 miles), 3hr

From the summit follow the signs towards Sommerain. After a few minutes waymarks point left along a footpath going down through the trees. Cross a track, and zigzag downhill, eventually emerging at a large clearing with a bench.

Turn left along the track, signed to Sommerain, then some minutes later, leave on a footpath to the left. At another forest track turn right, but once again leave on the left, following signs for Châtenois, and zigzagging down through beech woods. At the next track turn left, uphill, (ignoring the small path opposite) then take the right-hand fork. After about 0.4km leave to the right to descend past an enclosed water source.

Turn right towards Châtenois at a vehicle track, and when it turns sharply right, leave to the left. At a T-junction, turn right and very soon reach a road at Sommerain.

Turn right, then immediately left, but after about a hundred metres leave to the right between two forest plantations, then fork left within minutes. Continue through the woods, passing through open woodland allowing views of the distant hilltop castle of Haut-Koenigsbourg. After at least 1km this reaches the junction at Neue Matten.

Bernstein Castle

Turn left along a vehicle track to a road, cross the D253 and take the footpath to the right of the D203. At the next road do not take the path directly opposite, but turn right then immediately left down a wide path through trees, to the shelter at Teufelsloch. Leave by the lane opposite towards the Château Fort du Bernstein.

Turn left on a footpath that rejoins the lane a few minutes later, where the route takes a track to the left. Branch right, and at the next track, turn left to arrive at a rather oddly-shaped rock, the Rocher de l'Âne. Turn right, onto the footpath just beside it, to reach the parking area at Schulwaldplatz.

The tower provides a vantage point over the village of Dambach-la-Ville, where the line of the old ramparts can still be seen.

Leave by Chemin Forestier du Château, going steeply uphill, passing a shelter and a crucifix, then fork left and continue to **Bernstein Castle**. ◄

Bernstein Castle to Châtenois, 8.5km (5.5 miles), 2hr 30min

Hotels, gîte, restaurants, cafés and shops in Châtenois.

Leave Bernstein Castle towards Ortenbourg. At Kriegshurst take the path almost opposite, and after a very short distance leave to the left.

Take the track left at Rehhag, then fork right along a broad footpath. On joining a more major track follow it to the left. Turn right at a picnic site and take the path downhill. A short diversion to the left gives an excellent view of the white granite tower of **Ortenbourg Castle** from a higher level, but continuing down reaches another viewpoint looking up at the massive walls from below.

Turn right, downhill, and wind down to a road by a series of hairpins, passing close to **Ramstein Castle**, a single tower now in a dangerous condition. Turn right along the road, branch left, then turn left where waymarked, along a path twisting through scrub for nearly 2km before reaching the D35. Turn right and cross the bridge into **Châtenois**, crossing the N59 at a roundabout.

Châtenois to La Wick, 5km (3 miles), 1hr 30min

Café in La Wick.

Continue down the main street, passing Rue de l'Église, where a short diversion reaches the old town gates. After the narrowed section of road, leave along the next road to the right, towards the church, passing the gîte d'étape.

Keep to the left of the church, following waymarks along a track, then turn right along a road through vineyards. As this starts to drop back towards the town, branch left, entering woods. Turn left around a hairpin bend at Place du 1er Mai, and continue for about 25min along the side of a wooded valley.

When the main track hairpins left (blue circle route), carry straight on to Borne Pentagonale, a five-sided marker stone. Just beyond is a shelter, turn left towards La Wick. The high wire fence is the boundary of the **Montagne des Singes sanctuary** for Barbary apes. ▸

At La Wick there is a café by the entrance to the sanctuary.

**La Wick to Haut-Koenigsbourg,
4km (2.5 miles), 1hr 30min**
Café/restaurant and snack stall in Haut-Koenigsbourg.

Take a path into the woods on the right to skirt the car park, then turn right, along a forest track. Follow the route to Haut-Koenigsbourg, soon leaving to the left. The GR5 follows a footpath running parallel to the road to Borne

*Haut-Koenigsbourg
Castle*

81

Hexagonale. Fork left, and at Kreuzweg take the middle path towards Haut-Koenigsbourg. At the next junction, follow the main path to the left.

The path climbs quite steeply and meets the road. Cross over, then at a junction turn sharply right. Where the path meets a higher loop of the road, take the footpath almost opposite. This zigzags uphill, steeply in places, following signs to **Haut-Koenigsbourg**, until the castle buildings appear above.

> Although **Haut-Koenigsbourg Castle** stands on a site fortified from at least the 12th century, much of the building visible today dates from the beginning of the 20th century. The castle was taken by the Swedes in 1633 and substantially destroyed, the ruins eventually becoming the property of the town of Sélestat. In 1899 they were presented to Kaiser Wilhelm II, who decided to restore and furnish it in a representation of feudal style. The restoration may not be accurate in historical detail, but it is undoubtedly impressive.

Haut-Koenigsbourg to Thannenkirch, 4km (2.5 miles), 1hr 15min
Hotels, café/restaurants and shop in Thannenkirch.

Carry on along a broad footpath with the castle to the right, then continue downhill to cross two loops of the road. Keep straight on where tracks merge, to a junction near a large old house. Take the small footpath up the bank into the woods opposite.

Almost immediately, at a junction with two paths to the left, take the second, which curves round to run parallel with the D42 and stays within sight of this road, to pass behind the houses of the hamlet of **La Cave de Rodern**. Just beyond, cross a track and follow a footpath through the woods for over 1km, crossing several tracks, to reach a clearing with benches and a drinking water point. Turn right down the road, then take the minor road forking left to join the main road through **Thannenkirch**.

Thannenkirch to Ribeauvillé, 6km (3.5 miles), 2hr
Hotels, campsites, restaurants, cafés
and shops in Ribeauvillé.

Just beyond the village where the road hairpins left, leave on the track ahead. Fork left, then take a footpath climbing obliquely to the right. Follow it round the valley side to meet a track. Turn right and at a sharp bend to the left, take the upper track, towards Trois Châteaux.

On emerging onto a larger track, turn right to Ici les Quatre Chênes. Turn left, and after about 5min leave to the left, still towards 'les châteaux'. Turn left at a T-junction, then take the path ahead to the hilltop castle of **Haut-Ribeaupierre**, now in a dangerous condition.

From the gateway of Haut-Ribeaupierre continue down a steep, zigzagging path to the extensive ruins of the second castle, **St-Ulrich**. The route continues downhill, giving an excellent view of the third castle, **Girsberg**, on its rock promontory. Follow a distinct path that hairpins down, passing vineyards, with views over **Ribeauvillé**. Turn right, beside the town wall, to reach Place de la République. The town centre is down Grand'Rue to the left.

> **Ribeauvillé** lies at the edge of the Plain of Alsace, surrounded by vineyards and overlooked by the three ruined castles. The history of the town is strongly linked with the Lords of Ribeaupierre, a powerful family in Haute-Alsace. They came to prominence in the 13th century and their lands included Ste-Marie-aux-Mines, where silver mines generated huge wealth.
>
> Grand'Rue and the little backstreets on both sides are flanked by old buildings. Timber-framed houses dating to the 16th and 17th centuries are much in evidence, and the sole surviving town gate, the Porte des Bouchers, still stands astride a narrow cobbled street.

SECTION 5
GR5 RIBEAUVILLÉ TO MITTLACH

Ribeauvillé

This section includes one of the most popular stretches of the route in the Vosges. While the landscape is generally one of rounded hilltops, the high ridge that forms part of this walk has a rugged, east-facing cliff-line, with views over glacial lakes set in imposing cirques in the valley below.

The lively town of Ribeauvillé, with its flavour of old Alsace, provides a pleasant starting point. The footpath climbs through extensive woodland, and it comes as a surprise in this peaceful landscape to stumble over reminders of wartime. The remains of trenches and rusting tangles of barbed wire surrounding Tête des Faux are relics from World War I.

Beyond Col du Calvaire the path emerges from the cover of the trees onto the *hautes chaumes* (high pastures), with excellent views. The GR5 crosses the Réserve Naturelle de Tanet–Gazon du Faing, an area of forest, bog and grassland.

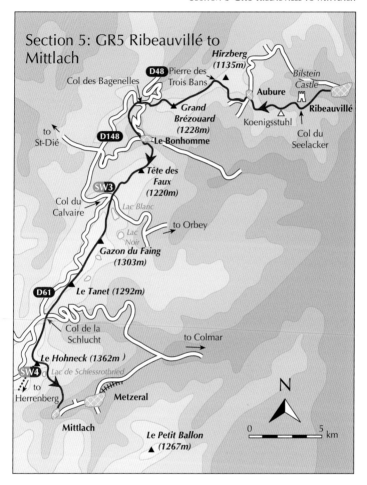

Section 5: GR5 Ribeauvillé to Mittlach

Col des Bagenelles
D48 Pierre des Trois Bans
Hirzberg (1135m)
Bilstein Castle
Aubure
Ribeauvillé
Koenigsstuhl
Col du Seelacker
to St-Dié
D148
Grand Brézouard (1228m)
Le Bonhomme
Tête des Faux (1220m)
SW3
Col du Calvaire
Lac Blanc
Lac Noir
to Orbey
Gazon du Faing (1303m)
D61
Le Tanet (1292m)
Col de la Schlucht
to Colmar
Le Hohneck (1362m)
SW4
Lac de Schiessrothried
to Herrenberg
Metzeral
Mittlach
Le Petit Ballon (1267m)
N
0   5 km

From here the landscape of the central Vosges can be appreciated, dominated by forested ridges with a scattering of villages in the valleys between.

For many kilometres between Col du Calvaire and Col de la Schlucht the path runs along the edge of cliffs with a series of lakes situated just to the east. Although there are some short, steep climbs, the walking along the ridge is easy.

Lac de Fischboedle

Le Hohneck, at 1362m, is the highest point reached on the GR5 so far, and an abrupt final descent reaches the Wormsa Valley. This is a good section of the walk for spotting chamois, but any disturbance will see them disappear.

This section can be walked in three days, with suggested stops at Le Bonhomme and Col de la Schlucht, finishing with an easy day to Mittlach.

SECTION SUMMARY TABLE			
Start	Distance	Ascent/Descent	Time
Ribeauvillé	10.5km (6.5 miles)	700m/140m	3hr 15min
Aubure	5km (3 miles)	330m/0m	1hr 30min
Pierre des Trois-Bans	10.5km (6.5 miles)	100m/540m	3hr 15min
Le Bonhomme	8km (5 miles)	540m/90m	2hr 45min
Col du Calvaire	10km (6 miles)	170m/170m	3hr 45min
Col de la Schlucht	10km (6 miles)	220m/830m	3hr 30min

SECTION 5
Ribeauvillé to Mittlach

Start	Ribeauvillé
Distance	54km (33.5 miles)
Maps	IGN TOP100 sheet 122; TOP75 sheet 028; Club Vosgien 1:50,000 sheet 6/8

Ribeauvillé to Aubure, 10.5km (6.5 miles), 3hr 15min
*Hotels, campsites, restaurants, cafés and shops
in Ribeauvillé; restaurant in Aubure.*

STORKS

Ribeauvillé is one of the places on the GR5 where storks are most likely to be seen. These elegant birds are symbols of prosperity and the emblem of Alsace. By the early 1970s the fall in numbers was so marked that in 1976 the Centre for the Reintroduction of Storks was set up in Hunawihr, 2km from Ribeauvillé. Storks migrate to Africa for the winter, and a huge proportion of them were not returning. The solution was to keep some of the birds in Alsace over the winter. From a low point of two breeding pairs in the whole of Alsace in 1982, numbers have increased to about 600 pairs.

These large black-and-white birds, with long red legs and beaks, are quite distinctive, and their nests on towers and chimney stacks are obvious. Despite the mess, having a stork's nest on the roof is considered lucky, and platforms are sometimes provided to encourage them.

From Place de la République go up Route de Ste-Marie-aux-Mines and turn left at a traffic island, then right along Rue St-Morand, and continue up through woodland. At an oblique path junction the GR5 turns sharply left. Avoid the yellow cross route ahead.

Follow the path as it hairpins up the hill, and connects with the end of a broad track, which continues to the clearing and pond at **Col du Seelacker**. Turn right, and at a slightly staggered crossroads go uphill, ahead, towards

The rock at Koenigsstuhl has two indentations, which with a bit of imagination can be used as seats. Nowadays the surrounding trees considerably restrict the view out across the valley.

Aubure. At a junction where **Bilstein Castle** is 300m off-route, the GR5 swings left, towards Koenigsstuhl.

The path reaches a tree labelled Sapin des Français. Take the footpath to the left which leads onto a track. Turn right, past a memorial cross, and fork left immediately beyond. Fork right, uphill, and where the track hairpins right, the route leaves towards Koenigsstuhl. Follow this path uphill and after about 15min, at the top of the rise, is a group of rocks with an inscription confirming that you have reached **Koenigsstuhl** (King's Seat). ◄

Follow the clear footpath down to a Club Vosgien memorial. Go slightly to the right of the picnic bench, cross an area of broken rocks, then fork right. At a major track, continue to the left.

At the next junction turn right, but almost immediately drop off the track onto a broad path. Fork left in a clearing, to come out onto a track which reaches a road. Follow to the right into **Aubure**, the highest village in Alsace. Fork left towards the church.

Aubure to Pierre des Trois-Bans, 5km (3 miles), 1hr 30min
Shelter at Pierre des Trois-Bans.

At the *mairie* (town hall) follow the road uphill to Col de Fréland. Turn right to pass a belvédère dating back to World War I. The route takes the second vehicle track to the right, Chemin Militaire, and where another track crosses diagonally, take the higher track ahead. After about 20min the route leaves by a minor fork to the right, towards Pierre des Trois-Bans. Almost immediately, fork right and continue to the shelter at **Pierre des Trois-Bans**. ◄

A short diversion reaches a nearby viewpoint.

Pierre des Trois-Bans to Le Bonhomme, 10.5km (6.5 miles), 3hr 15min
Refuge and ferme-auberge at Col des Bagenelles; hotels, campsite, gîte, restaurants, café/ bar and shops in Le Bonhomme.

Go left from the clearing, roughly following a ridge-line through the forest. Leave to the right, following signs to Brézouard. Less than 10min later watch out for a little path on the left, going uphill onto the granite top of Petit Brézouard.

Pierre des Trois-Bans, shelter

The path dips down, past an unlocked Club Vosgien shelter, then rises onto the next hilltop. Take the narrow path opposite to the summit of **Grand Brézouard** (1228m). Turn right and descend to cross a parking area, then continue uphill almost opposite and fork left. This passes one of the more unusual relics of World War I, a preserved mosaic of German military insignia.

At the next track, turn right, and soon left to follow the track to **Col des Bagenelles**. Go left along the D48, and just beyond the junction with the D148, turn right into a lane. Immediately take a footpath left down through a field to a lane, turn left, and at the next corner, leave down a track on the right to join the D48. Turn right, and very soon turn right, down a footpath through woodland. After crossing the road again, fork right onto a footpath to **Le Bonhomme**.

Le Bonhomme to Col du Calvaire,
8km (5 miles), 2hr 45min
Hotel/gîte at Étang du Devin; hotel, refuge
and café/restaurant at Col du Calvaire.

Continue into the village, go left down the main road, and turn right by the mairie. The path climbs abruptly to a lane. Turn left, uphill, passing the gîte and campsite. Turn right at the first junction, left up a footpath into woodland, then carry straight on along tracks for about 1.5km to reach a junction by a small former military cemetery. Turn right and continue to Étang du Devin, a quiet lake surrounded by trees. Follow the footpath opposite the World War I shelter, climbing steeply through conifer woodland.

> The path passes another military building, a former **German ammunition depot** where munitions were winched up to the lines at the top of the ridge. A few old photographs inside the building give an idea of how things once looked.

Pass Roche du Corbeau and fork right, towards Tête des Faux, to climb to the Panorama des Alpes, although distant mountain views may be hidden by mist.

Throughout this area, it is advisable to keep to paths to avoid wartime debris hidden in the vegetation, and deep pits and collapsed tunnels among the ruins. At the summit of **Tête des Faux** (1220m), the route passes the remains of trenches and rusty barbed wire from World War I.

> Soon after the outbreak of war, the Germans established an artillery command post on **Tête des Faux**. The French saw the nearby Col du Bonhomme as a potential approach for their assault on Colmar and needed control of the heights alongside. They attacked in strength, and using crack mountain troops, the Chasseurs Alpins, together with a battalion of infantry, seized the area and dug in. The

Germans counterattacked, but could not retake the summit. These front-line positions became fixed for the rest of the war.

On the hillside today the trenches remain, often hewn into the rock, with opposing front lines sometimes within a few dozen metres. There is a memorial to the Chasseurs Alpins.

The path downhill passes over a cobbled section of track which once formed a wartime supply route. ▸ Continue through the woods to a more major forest track, and follow this left to **Col du Calvaire**.

At Carrefour Duchesne, the information board at the military cemetery details the nearby battle fronts.

Col du Calvaire to Col de la Schlucht, 10km (6 miles), 3hr 45min

Ferme-auberge in Gazon du Faing (0.5km off-route); auberge/hotel in Schanzwasen (1.5km off-route); hotel and restaurants at Col de la Schlucht.

Cross the D48 by the chalet-style café/restaurant and turn left, but after a few metres, leave to the right. This footpath reaches a clearing where the route turns right and climbs steadily.

Lac Blanc, far below, can be glimpsed between the trees. Within about 1km fork right, to reach the open hilltop where an information board marks the entrance to the Réserve Naturelle de Tanet–Gazon du Faing.

The path climbs up onto a broad ridge with views opening out in both directions.

Occasional eroded **boundary stones** on this section of the path have an 'F' on the west and a 'D' (Deutschland) on the east, marking the border fixed at the end of the Franco-Prussian War in 1871. The land to the east remained part of Germany until the end of World War I.

The route follows a well-worn path. A short detour to the left offers a view over **Lac Blanc**, but the main route carries on. Within half an hour this reaches a signpost

Lac Blanc

where the path left goes to **Lac Noir**, but the GR5 continues towards Col de la Schlucht. After a few hundred metres, the route bends right where the land beyond falls steeply away. Continue to the signpost at **Gazon du Faing** (1303m).

The land to the left drops away in a series of cliffs and rocky headlands, and the views extend towards the valley of the Rhine. ◄

Turn right, following the signs towards Col de la Schlucht. The next few kilometres provide excellent walking as the path follows the crest.

Pass an impressive rock, the Taubenklangfelsen, to reach a final rocky high point at Ringbuhlkopf, where there is an option of taking an alternative route for a short distance. Both routes drop down to the D61 about 1km later. This road is the Route des Crêtes, originally built for military purposes, but now providing a tourist drive along the crest of the Vosges. The GR5 leaves on the far side of a car park towards Col de la Schlucht.

The path climbs over a rocky prominence at Roche du Tanet by the summit of **Le Tanet** (1292m). Carry on, passing a sign indicating the route to Schanzwasen Auberge. After Haut de Baerenbach, descend by a rocky path to the D417 at **Col de la Schlucht** (1139m).

Col de la Schlucht to Mittlach,
10km (6 miles), 3hr 30min
Refuge/gîte and ferme-auberge in Trois-Fours;
restaurant and auberge/hotels in Le Hohneck; ferme-
auberge in Schiessroth; hotels and shops in Metzeral
(3km off-route); chambres d'hôtes in Mittlach.

Turn right, along the road, then left up a lane beside a souvenir shop. Go left again almost immediately and follow up to the left of the church. Continue uphill, forking left to keep near the edge of the ridge. The path emerges into open meadows with the Alps on the skyline. At a road, where a signpost indicates Chalet des Trois-Fours to the left, turn right, towards Le Hohneck. Look out for a footpath leaving to the left and follow it as it rises up the ridge, with steepening cliffs to the left, to Col de Falimont. It is possible in summer to take an alternative GR5 path skirting the side of Le Hohneck to rejoin the route at Col du Schaeferthal, but the main route carries on, then turns uphill to the summit (turn off here for the Refuge du Sotré at Haut-Chitelet).

Ascent of Le Hohneck

CHAMOIS

The slopes around Le Hohneck are favourite haunts of chamois. Eleven animals from the Black Forest were released at Ranspach, near Le Markstein, in 1956, since when the population has grown substantially, with some 800 to 1000 animals in the Southern Vosges today. To avoid tree damage, controlled hunting is allowed to limit numbers to these levels.

Before the early 1980s chamois had no natural predators in the Vosges, although since then introduced lynx may take a few animals, but increasing disturbance from people may also influence local populations.

The top of **Le Hohneck** (1362m) is the highest point in the immediate vicinity with an impressive panorama from the summit restaurant and terrace.

A shorter, high-level alternative route with red-white-red waymarking takes the path that goes south from Le Hohneck. It skirts Le Kastelberg (1346m) and Le Rainkopf to follow the ridge before rejoining the main GR5 at Col du Herrenberg (Section 6) after 7.5km.

However, the main GR5 route descends in the direction of Schaeferthal, leaving to the right of the telescope and dropping fairly steeply to the Col du Schaeferthal. Turn right and follow a rocky path downhill to the ferme-auberge of Schiessroth. Take the footpath dropping beside the building, with Lac de Schiessrothried encircled by the valley below, and continue down a series of hairpin bends.

Turn right to **Lac de Schiessrothried**, cross the dam, and immediately turn left, towards Fischboedle. Descend beside the stream to Lac de Fischboedle, a little lake known for its picturesque setting.

Turn left at the lake, and follow a broad path downhill, turn left again where this meets a track, then look out soon afterwards for a right turn onto a forest footpath, following a ledge in the hillside. When the route meets a small track, it veers to the right along it, emerging onto pastureland.

The GR5 diverges here – to the right the primary route goes to Mittlach, while the left fork forms a spur

to **Metzeral**. If you are looking for a food shop, you will find Metzeral, 3km off-route, more useful. To stay with the main path, turn right and follow signs to **Mittlach**.

Looking over Schaeferthal

Mittlach dates back to the 16th and 17th centuries, when it was settled by Tyrolean lumberjacks and iron miners, giving it a shorter history than many of the other villages in the region. Forestry continues to be important in the district today, but the iron deposits are no longer exploited. Mittlach escaped major damage in World War I, although nearby Metzeral was right on the front line and was totally destroyed.

95

SECTION 6
GR5 MITTLACH TO THANN

The old town of Thann

This section includes Le Grand Ballon, the highest point of the Vosges. Easy road access means that the summit region may be busy, although elsewhere along the ridge the path is left to hikers.

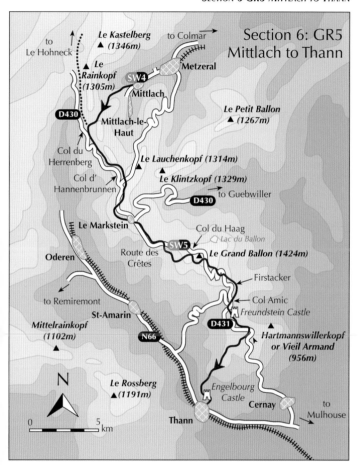

to Le Hohneck

Le Kastelberg ▲ (1346m)

to Colmar →

Section 6: GR5 Mittlach to Thann

▲ *Le Rainkopf (1305m)*

SW4

Metzeral

Mittlach

Le Petit Ballon ▲ (1267m)

Mittlach-le-Haut

D430

Col du Herrenberg

Le Lauchenkopf (1314m) ▲

Col d' Hannenbrunnen

Le Klintzkopf (1329m) ▲

→ to Guebwiller

D430

● **Le Markstein**

Col du Haag

Lac du Ballon

Oderen

SW5

Route des Crêtes

Le Grand Ballon (1424m) ▲

Firstacker

to Remiremont

Col Amic

Freundstein Castle

St-Amarin

D431

Mittelrainkopf (1102m) ▲

N66

Hartmannswillerkopf or Vieil Armand (956m) ▲

N

Le Rossberg ▲ (1191m)

Engelbourg Castle

0   5 km

Cernay

Thann

to Mulhouse

Most of the climbing for this stretch of the walk is tackled soon after leaving Mittlach, when about 600m is gained over 4km. At the top of this ascent the route leaves the forest behind, then runs along the ridge roughly parallel with the quiet tourist road of the Route des Crêtes. There are many lookout points over the wooded valleys below, and fermes-auberges provide refreshment opportunities at several of the cols.

Le Grand Ballon is worth visiting to see the immense view, and a panorama board names points of interest out to the horizon. The descent is mainly through forest, passing the ruins of Freundstein Castle, and further on, the World War I cemetery at Hartmannswillerkopf. A thought-provoking detour from here on a short loop trail leads through many of the trenches and fortifications of the old battlefield.

On finally dropping down into the valley, the path passes Engelbourg Castle and the unusual Oeil de la Sorcière (Witch's Eye) to reach the small town of Thann.

This section can be walked in two days, with a suggested stop at Le Markstein or the hotel on Le Grand Ballon.

SECTION SUMMARY TABLE

Start	Distance	Ascent/Descent	Time
Mittlach	6km (4 miles)	660m/0m	2hr 30min
Col du Herrenberg	8.5km (5.5 miles)	20m/0m	2hr 35min
Le Markstein	8.5km (5.5 miles)	230m/20m	2hr 35min
Le Grand Ballon	5km (3 miles)	0m/590m	1hr 30min
Col Amic	3.5km (2 miles)	100m/30m	1hr
Vieil Armand	9km (5.5 miles)	160m/720m	3hr

SECTION 6
Mittlach to Thann

Start	Mittlach
Distance	40.5km (25 miles)
Maps	IGN TOP100 sheet 122; TOP75 sheet 028; Club Vosgien 1:50,000 sheet 6/8

Mittlach to Col du Herrenberg, 6km (4 miles), 2hr 30min

Chambres d'hôtes in Mittlach; ferme-auberge at Col du Herrenberg.

From the centre of Mittlach go up Rue Raymond Poincaré and cross a stream. The GR5 leaves to the right beside a noticeboard, where a footpath climbs into the woods. After a few minutes cross over a major track, then turn left along a broad grassy track, to follow it as it hairpins uphill.

Mittlach-le-Haut

Keep zigzagging upwards, and after about 40min, follow waymarks up a steep verge. This joins a broad forestry track on a hairpin bend, where there is an excellent view back over **Mittlach-le-Haut**. Take the forest track uphill, passing a crossroads at Chemin des Italiens. Pass Chemin des Souilles and go over the next junction, passing Chemin Renault. Follow this stony track, to leave the forest at an access gap, cross a strip of pasture, then turn left along the forest edge.

VOSGIENNE

On the high pastures in summer the walker will see many cattle. The Vosgienne is one breed worth noticing, as it is unique to this part of France. A small cow, usually speckled black and white, Vosgienne were introduced into France in the 17th century and were once widespread in the Vosges, but numbers dwindled. Plans to develop the breed were put in place in the 1970s and the decline was reversed. These cows are valued for their hardiness and ability to thrive in hill conditions, and for the quality of their milk. The many local cheeses, including the well-known Munster cheese, owe a great deal to the little Vosgienne.

Carry on for a few minutes to a gate onto a vehicle track. Turn left and look for a footpath to the right, down through a short section of open woodland, then across pastureland to **Col du Herrenberg**. The **Route des Crêtes** (D430) and the ferme-auberge of Huss lie just ahead, and the high-level route from Le Hohneck (Section 5) rejoins from the right.

Col du Herrenberg to Le Markstein,
8.5km (5.5 miles), 2hr 35min
Ferme-auberge at Col d'Hannenbrunnen; hotels, gîte, refuges and café/restaurants in Le Markstein.

Turn left on the signposted footpath to the high point of Schweisel. Carry on along this path for about half an hour, crossing over a path junction, then a tractor track. Follow an obvious path to the right, skirting the next summit. Turn left along the D430 to pass the Touring Club Mulhouse refuge and reach **Col d'Hannenbrunnen**. Leave the road to the left, towards Le Markstein.

At Le Breitfirst cross the D27, then the D430, and continue along the path, which cuts off a bend then follows the curve of the road. The GR5 skirts **Le Markstein**, then joins the road at the end of the village.

> **Le Markstein** is a small, modern ski resort, functional rather than picturesque. It provides a useful centre for accommodation and refreshments, although there is no shop for provisions.

Le Markstein to Le Grand Ballon, 8.5km (5.5 miles), 2hr 35min
Ferme-auberge at Col du Haag; hotel and restaurants/cafés at Le Grand Ballon.

Turn right and cross a junction onto the D431, signposted to Le Grand Ballon. The footpath keeps to the left-hand side of this road, shadowing it for about 3km before rejoining it. Cross the road and drop downhill to a track. After only a few minutes look out for a fork up to the left. Do not continue with the main track downhill towards St-Amarin.

Ignore minor paths, and carry straight on where a major track joins from the right. The summit of Le Grand Ballon, with its radar dome, suddenly appears, looming above.

> From the slopes of Le Grand Ballon the effect of **temperature inversion** is sometimes an impressive spectacle. When a layer of colder air is trapped in the valleys, the result is a sea of cloud across the lower ground, with the hilltops of the Vosges appearing as islands breaking through to the sunshine above.

Turn left along a road to the junction at **Col du Haag**, passing the Ferme-Auberge du Haag. The GR5 goes

Towards the summit of Le Grand Ballon

to the right, following a footpath which climbs steadily and curves around the south side of the summit. It then turns sharply, and it is a short climb to the top of **Le Grand Ballon** (1424m), following a section of the Circuit Panoramique.

> The radar dome on **Le Grand Ballon** is visible for a considerable distance, and the panorama board on the terrace is worth a visit. Slightly downhill is the Diables Bleus memorial, commemorating a division of the French army who fought here in World War I. Further down, the scant remains of the old hotel can still be seen near the present Hôtel du Grand Ballon. This hotel is run by the Club Vosgien, a long-standing organisation for walkers, so despite its rather grand appearance, walkers are welcome and a reasonably priced set meal is usually available.

Le Grand Ballon to Col Amic, 5km (3 miles), 1hr 30min
Ferme-auberge at Ferme du Ballon.

Descend from the summit dome along the broad walkway, then follow the footpath to the road at the Chalet-Hôtel du Grand Ballon. Turn right, towards Col Amic, and just beyond a ski-lift, look out for a waymark indicating a footpath to the left, which continues down a ski run for over 1km. Ahead is the plain of Alsace with its scattering of towns and villages. Head down to a large building with a red roof, the Ferme-Auberge du Grand Ballon.

Cross the road twice before descending into beech wood and continuing towards Firstacker. The path reaches a T-junction where the left-hand route is to Judenhut, but the GR5 goes right to come out at **Firstacker**. ▶

Go down to a vehicle track and follow an earth track almost opposite, which curves into woodland. Very soon the GR5 takes a small footpath to the right that drops down and runs parallel to the Route des Crêtes, before reaching **Col Amic**.

On the hillside opposite is a World War I memorial chapel, with a tricolour flying beside it.

Col Amic to Vieil Armand, 3.5km (2 miles), 1hr

Leave through the picnic area on the opposite side of the road, and a few minutes later come out on another road where the route to Chapelle Sicurani, (yellow triangle) is opposite, but the GR5 turns right. Look out for a footpath on the left and take this to the ruins of **Freundstein Castle**.

At 984m **Freundstein** is the highest of the many castles of the Vosges. In the ownership of the same family from at least the 13th century, it was severely damaged by lightning in 1526, and soon after abandoned as the family home. As a military building it was last used as an observation post in World War I, and heavily bombarded as a result.

The GR5 dips downhill through hazel wood, and comes within sight of the road, but bears left past a sign for the Ferme-Auberge Freundstein and climbs into the woods. The footpath cuts into the side of the hill, and continues round the head of a valley. Follow the well-used path along the side of this wooded slope. The route emerges onto the D431 close to the entrance to the memorial of **Hartmannswillerkopf (Vieil Armand)**.

The memorial at **Hartmannswillerkopf** is a low, grey, stone building with the main door flanked by two massive statues. A rock-cut crypt contains the remains of 12,000 unknown soldiers, and a cemetery lies behind.

There was fierce fighting in the area as both sides attempted to hold the high ground overlooking the Belfort Gap. During various offensives in 1915 and early 1916 the summit changed hands eight times. Neither side was able to claim a decisive victory, and the battle lines remained static until the armistice.

The name Vieil Armand was given to the hill by French soldiers, who found the local Germanic name difficult to pronounce. The hilltop battlefield, now marked with a 20m-tall cross, may be visited by taking a short detour from the GR5, and a walking trail leads through the old front lines, where trenches and bunkers are particularly well preserved.

Vieil Armand to Thann, 9km (5.5 miles), 3hr
Refuge and ferme-auberge/refuge in Molkenrain; hotels, gîte, restaurants, cafés and shops in Thann.

Turn left down the road, passing the memorial, and take the track immediately beyond a fontaine (not drinking water) on the right. At a signpost, take a footpath to the right and climb steadily, turn left at a stone marker-post and follow across pasture, soon meeting the end of a road. Fork right towards the Ferme-Auberge du Molkenrain, an excellent place to enjoy refreshments and take in the view across the valley. Immediately beyond, follow the footpath to the right, straight up the hillside behind the farmhouse.

At the top of the field go through an access gap, and take the track to the right, to a Les Amis de la Nature refuge. Leave by a footpath, signposted to Thann, beside a wooden water trough. Follow the marked trail downhill through the woods, crossing several tracks and passing a sign to a viewpoint, just off-route.

Camp Turenne is a clearing in the forest, with a short diversion to the viewpoint at Rocher d'Ostein, but the GR5 continues to the right of a World War I memorial, on a track signposted 'Thann par ruines d'Engelbourg'.

At Camp des Pyramides go straight across the cross-roads, following the sign to Thann – this path is quite stony underfoot at points, as it descends through the forest. At the next clearing, go straight on to Col du Grumbach.

The GR5 takes the route via the ruins of Engelbourg Castle. Follow the Route Forestière du Rosenbourg out of the clearing, and a short way down there is a sharp turn to the right, still following the signs to Thann and Engelbourg.

After about 10min, shortly after the track turns sharply to the left, turn right along a woodland footpath and descend by a series of hairpins. Turn left at a junction to reach **Engelbourg Castle**, set on a high mound. The GR5 turns sharply left, but the easiest way to visit the ruins is to carry on round the bottom of the mound, past an information board, then take the path up to the castle.

The ruins of **Engelbourg Castle**, dating from the 13th century, are quite extensive, although none of the walls have survived to any great height. The most notable feature is the Oeil de la Sorcière

Oeil de la Sorcière

105

(Witch's Eye). When the castle was demolished in the 17th century, a massive piece of tower landed intact on its side – the result is a huge vertical circle of stonework with a round hole through the middle. It has been heavily repointed to keep it intact, but it is quite striking nevertheless.

From the terrace in front of the castle there is a fine outlook over Thann with its large Gothic church.

◂ On returning to the GR5 turn right, then look out for a sharp right down concrete steps to reach the edge of **Thann**. Follow Rue Marsilly, crossing straight over Place des Alliés, and continuing along this narrow street. Turn left over the River Thur at the first bridge and go past the local museum, to reach the centre of town.

People have been walking to **Thann** for far longer than the GR5 has existed, as the church of St-Thiébaut was a popular destination for pilgrimages in the Middle Ages. This church, which dates from the 14th to 16th centuries, is one of the most richly decorated in all of Alsace, and its west doorway is particularly striking.

Other attractions in Thann include several fine Renaissance houses and two medieval towers which once formed part of the town wall. The survival of these buildings is remarkable, as the town was heavily bombarded during both world wars. Another survival from the past is the half-pagan, half-Christian annual tradition of the Crémation des Trois Sapins, in which three fir trees are set alight.

SECTION 7
GR5 THANN TO BRÉVILLIERS

Étang by Malsaucy

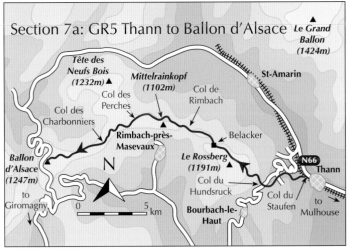

Section 7a: GR5 Thann to Ballon d'Alsace

This section sees the GR5 passing through areas of the Western Vosges which are less accessible, and less visited. After crossing the summit of Ballon d'Alsace, the route drops out of the Vosges into a flatter landscape of lakes, woods and small villages.

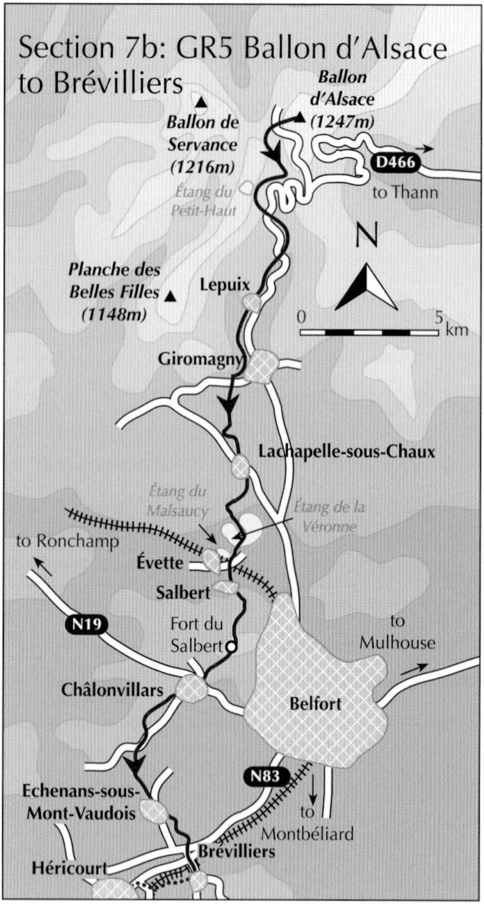

Much of the route up from Thann is wooded, with a sprinkling of remote fermes-auberges on the high pastures. While height has to be gained to leave the Thur Valley, the climbing is for the most part gradual. Deep, wooded valleys and isolated lakes make this a very attractive area, and the view over Lac des Perches, a magnificently sited glacial lake, is particularly memorable.

The high point of this section is the crossing of Ballon d'Alsace, at 1247m. The last few hundred metres of the climb are quite steep, but the effort is rewarded as the view is excellent. South from the Ballon the route descends from the Vosges to the village of Giromagny and passes Fort Dorsner, then climbs to the hilltop site of Fort du Salbert, before reaching Brévilliers across the flatter land of the Belfort Gap.

Above the Doller Valley

Choice of accommodation is restricted in this section, but we suggest three days' walking, with overnight stops at Rouge Gazon and Giromagny, although the final day is long.

SECTION SUMMARY TABLE			
Start	Distance	Ascent/Descent	Time
Thann	6.5km (4 miles)	410m/0m	2hr
Col du Hundsruck	6km (3.5 miles)	430m/200m	2hr
Belacker	6km (3.5 miles)	260m/180m	2hr
Col des Perches	8km (5 miles)	240m/50m	3hr 15min
Ballon d'Alsace	11km (7 miles)	0m/750m	3hr 20min
Lepuix	2km (1 mile)	0m/15m	30min
Giromagny	7km (4.5 miles)	100m/180m	2hr
Lachapelle-sous-Chaux	4km (2.5 miles)	0m/0m	1hr 15min
Évette	4km (2.5 miles)	250m/0m	1hr 15min
Fort du Salbert	4.5km (3 miles)	30m/290m	1hr 15min
Châlonvillars	6km (3.5 miles)	20m/30m	2hr
Échenans-sous-Mont-Vaudois	3.5km (2 miles)	0m/20m	1hr

SECTION 7
Thann to Brévilliers

Start	Thann
Distance	68.5km (42.5 miles)
Maps	IGN TOP100 sheet 31; TOP75 sheet 028; Club Vosgien 1:50,000 sheet 7/8

Thann to Col du Hundsruck, 6.5km (4 miles), 2hr
Hotels, gîte, restaurants, cafés and shops in Thann; hotel/restaurant at Col du Hundsruck.

At the church, turn left along Rue de la Première Armée, and right along the first main road, Rue Kléber. Cross the N66, then a level crossing, and take the first road on the right, Rue des Jardins. The gîte is further along Rue Kléber.

Turn right along Chemin du Staufen, and follow it as the climb out of the valley of the Thur begins. The road ends, and the GR5 continues up the hill along a pleasant little track. After less than 1km, follow a waymarked path to the right to **Col du Staufen**.

Turn left along Route Forestière Roi de Rome, and pass a sign for Croix de Mission. Take a small footpath dropping to the left, which joins a track to Place du Roi de Rome. Leave along the track opposite. Within a couple of kilometres this emerges onto a road.

Turn left, passing a wooden shelter at Plan Diebolt Scherrer then leave to the left, just beyond the junction, taking a path zigzagging upwards through beech woods. After about 1km the path skirts a rocky section above a road and then descends to **Col du Hundsruck**. The small auberge here provides accommodation rather than casual refreshments.

Col du Hundsruck to Belacker, 6km (3.5 miles), 2hr
Ferme-auberge/refuge at Thannerhubel (off-route); ferme-auberge/gîte at Belacker.

Cross the road onto a footpath following along the side of a wooded valley. Within 1km the path reaches the edge of pasture where the GR5 divides. ▶ The main GR5 route is signed ahead to Belacker.

Immediately after the junction, the path crosses a track, then merges with a more major track. Carry on in roughly the same direction. The view opens out over the summits of the Southern Vosges.

On leaving the wood, turn left along a vehicle track. The route crosses onto hilltop pastures, and ahead on the skyline is the Ski Club Rossberg refuge. The track leads past this chalet to Col du Rossberg. (The fermes-auberges of Le Rossberg and Thannerhubel lie off-route here.)

Go through the access point and continue left to a signpost where the GR5 branches obliquely right. Just below is the Ski Club Mulhouse refuge, with an accessible water supply.

Within 15min the track forks. Left is Wegscheid par Sattel, Fuchsfels. The route takes the right fork, even though waymarks may not be apparent, and soon an odd-shaped rock comes into view ahead just to the left of the GR. The hilltops in the distance are mostly tree-covered, but for the moment the route continues along one of the infrequent stretches of open ridge.

The onward path soon crosses a belt of beech wood. The ferme-auberge of Gsang is signed to the right, but the GR5 continues ahead. Pass a prominent lookout rock, the Vogelstein, with views over the Doller Valley, then lose height to reach an oblique T-junction and turn right.

The path winds down towards some farm buildings, the ferme-auberge of **Belacker**. At an elevation of close to 1000m, this is an excellent refreshment stop, popular with walkers but not accessible by public road. One part of this working farm is now a gîte d'étape.

Belacker to Col des Perches, 6km (3.5 miles), 2hr

Past Belacker, take the uphill direction of the hairpin for a short distance, then leave by a gate on the right, with open grassland beyond. Avoid the left turn to Wegscheid,

An alternative route leaves to the right and passes the ferme-auberge of Thannerhubel before rejoining in about 2km.

Approaching Belacker

and take the main path, curving left and keeping to much the same level.

Over the next kilometre this footpath provides fine views to the south. The woods close in again before reaching **Col de Rimbach**, a junction with a tiny shelter, where the GR5 goes straight on. A short distance beyond, leave by a footpath to the left, looking out for a sign on the tree opposite. On reaching a track, turn left and follow uphill for about half an hour, then climb a small flight of metal steps onto the headland of Rimbachkopf.

Some time later, the path hairpins sharply left, then zigzags uphill to keep fairly high through the woods, not too far below the ridge. This path is easily followed towards the junction at **Col des Perches**. On the approach to the col a brief open area allows a glimpse of the steeply wooded face of the cirque ahead, before the final descent to the col.

Col des Perches to Ballon d'Alsace, 8km (5 miles), 3hr 15min

Auberge/hotel/gîte at Rouge Gazon (1km off-route); shelter at Petite Chaume (0.3km off-route); hotel, ferme-auberge/ chambres d'hôtes and restaurant at Ballon d'Alsace.

At the col, the auberge/gîte of Gazon Vert is indicated to the right, while the GR5 carries on ahead. ▸ The rough path continues around the wooded bowl forming the backdrop to the lake, passing another viewpoint.

The path leaves the cirque and crosses a stretch of pasture before merging with a track coming from Rouge Gazon, with the GR5 carrying on ahead, passing a sign to a nearby spring. Within minutes the route is back into woodland and a small stream flows across the path.

About 5min later, while the main track twists down in an S-bend, the GR5 follows a direct line, cutting off two corners before leaving at a prominent signpost.

The path crosses a clearing then heads into steeply sloping woods to emerge at **Col des Charbonniers**. Cross another track and continue along the footpath opposite. About 15min later, look out for a GR waymark leading to the left while a short alternative route to a viewpoint continues on ahead, and rejoins soon afterwards.

Not far beyond a viewpoint and picnic table, the path to Petite Chaume, an accessible shelter a short distance off-route, is signposted to the right. Some 20min later, a second path from Petite Chaume joins from the right, and the GR5 keeps with the main path.

The surrounding woodland becomes noticeably rockier, and at Col de Morteville the trees are among tumbles of boulders. Within a few minutes the footpath snakes its way around rocks and zigzags upwards.

Some 10min later, the path crosses the open hilltop of Rundkopf where the Ballon d'Alsace comes into view – steep sided with an extended flat top. At a junction, the left branch is signed to Boedelen (refuge), but the GR5 takes the higher fork.

Pass the path to La Jumenterie, and in a few minutes a much closer view of the eastern slope of the Ballon is revealed, but there is still a steep uphill section to tackle before the summit. The path takes a zigzag line up between rocks and tree roots and is hard going with a heavy pack.

The climb reaches a level footpath on the summit plateau of the **Ballon d'Alsace**. There is a car park nearby,

The col is surrounded by trees, but an area of scree allows a bird's-eye view of Lac des Perches.

so it is likely that there will be other visitors, especially in summer.

The **Ballon d'Alsace** is the highest point in the Southern Vosges, and an excellent vantage point. Collectors of odd facts may be interested to learn that for a short distance you are walking along the watershed between the North Sea and the Mediterranean.

The statue of Joan of Arc dates back to 1909, when Alsace was still part of Germany and the Ballon was right at the edge of France, so it was erected to symbolise the attachment that France had for the lands of Alsace.

Cross to the viewpoint indicator, then turn right to follow waymarks around the plateau, passing the statue of Joan of Arc. From now on, the GR5 is marked with red and white waymarks. ◄ Follow the broad path down from the statue to the road, close to a café and tourist office.

Be aware that the red rectangle waymarks do continue to the south, but mark a route down to Belfort, not the main GR5 route.

From the Ballon d'Alsace

Ballon d'Alsace to Lepuix, 11km (7 miles), 3hr 20min
Chambres d'hôtes in Malvaux, shop in Lepuix.

Descent of the Ballon d'Alsace

The GR5 leaves through a car park beside a dramatic memorial to those who died clearing World War II mines. Note that the GR5 to Giromagny has changed, and maps may still show the former route. Initially, it joins with the GR7 and GR59 and drops through trees to a junction where the other GRs go right, but the GR5 forks left, towards Chalet Bonaparte. Follow this path for over a kilometre to a junction at a hairpin bend. Continue round to the right, towards the small lake of **Étang du Petit-Haut**. Keep on downhill, following waymarks. The descent becomes rockier before reaching the little lake.

Turn right, along the side of the lake, then leave to the left, beside a stream which tumbles by a series of rapids and waterfalls through a narrow wooded gorge. ▶ The path emerges near the Hôtel du Saut de la Truite (currently closed), and the route continues down a gravel track signed to Lepuix. This follows the River Savoureuse, curving right along a grassy track, to reach the end of a lane.

Viewing platforms overlook the more spectacular sections.

From here until Giromagny, the GR5 continues along the bottom of the valley. Follow the lane to a parking area, and take a footpath through woods to the left. Cross a footbridge, passing in front of a waterworks, to come out onto a road. Turn left briefly before leaving to the right just before Roche du Cerf. The route skirts the hamlet of Malvaux, following a series of tracks, paths and lanes to reach a road close to a sports field.

Continue down the road, and soon a sign points left along a footpath, by the side of woods. This leads back towards the Savoureuse, then turns to follow downstream, with the village of **Lepuix** ahead.

Lepuix to Giromagny, 2km (1 mile), 30min
Hotel, gîte, restaurants, cafés and shops in Giromagny.

On entering the village, turn left down Rue du Moulin and cross the square. Turn right after a small bridge, then very soon left to join a track crossing fields. Continue in roughly the same direction until a sign directs the route left, and the path joins a road at the edge of **Giromagny**. Turn left, then left again at a junction where Rue du Querty goes right. At the next junction, turn left, downhill, then within a few dozen metres fork right along a road heading towards a church spire. At a junction with a more major road, turn right, and continue to the D12.

> **Giromagny** lies at the heart of a mineral-rich region where mining began in the 14th century. The golden age was in the second half of the 16th century, when silver, copper and other metals were extracted from ever-deeper excavations, but mineral extraction ended by 1800.
>
> The Fort de Giromagny, Fort Dorsner, on the GR5 a few kilometres beyond the town, like Fort du Salbert (see later in this section), was built by the French in the 1870s to defend the Belfort area. The fort is only open to the public on limited occasions.

Giromagny to Lachapelle-sous-Chaux, 7km (4.5 miles), 2hr
Chambres d'hôtes in Lachapelle-sous-Chaux.

A left turn reaches the town centre but the GR5 turns right, then right again along Rue des Carrières. At the end of the buildings, follow waymarks left, down to the main road. Take the quiet lane opposite towards Fort Dorsner for about a kilometre, then leave to the left along a way-marked footpath leading around the perimeter of the fortifications.

On reaching the small parking area, turn left down a track and continue downhill for nearly half a kilometre. Follow signs right and continue along a forestry track, looping downhill. This track then leads through grassland, passing a series of small lakes, to reach a road. Turn left, but look out for a sign pointing right and follow a footpath through farmland towards **Lachapelle-sous-Chaux**.

Lachapelle-sous-Chaux to Évette, 4km (2.5 miles), 1hr 15min
Restaurant and café/bar in Évette.

On entering the village turn right, and cross a bridge onto Rue de la Libération, then turn left at a traffic island down Rue de Bellevue. At a bend with three tracks leaving to the right, take the left-hand one. Ahead is a distinct wooded hill topped by a mast, the site of Fort du Salbert, still two hours walk away. Follow the gravel track, where a series of lakes comes into view on the left.

Continue for about 1.5km, ignoring side paths. The track then turns right, passing a birdwatching hide, and stays beside the **Étang de la Véronne** until almost reaching a road. Turn right, still keeping to the waterside, then just beyond a car park, branch off to cross parkland to reach the **Étang du Malsaucy** and continue with the lake on the right.

Évette to Fort du Salbert, 4km (2.5 miles), 1hr 15min

Pass the Auberge du Lac and carry on into **Évette**, crossing the railway. Keep with the major road, and then turn left along Rue du Val, which becomes Chemin du Verboté.

The auberge at Évette

Turn right at a signpost where the GR533 and a GR5 access route to Belfort lie ahead. After passing house number eight fork left, and in a very short distance turn right, then left onto the D24. Turn right, along Rue de la Vierge towards Châlonvillars.

Pass Rue de la Fontaine, then immediately take a track to the left. After just a few metres, take a footpath left. Follow this as it curves round to an earth vehicle track where the route turns sharply right. Continue steeply uphill, following waymarks, until reaching a wooden footbridge to the right. Cross this and climb the steps to the top of **Fort du Salbert**.

> Built in 1875 **Fort du Salbert** is one of a chain of a dozen similar forts that encircle Belfort. All date from the 1874 to 1914 period and were raised following the shock of the Prussian victory in 1871. Each fort sheltered infantry and artillery and provided an interconnecting defensive shield around the town. These forts are now mostly overgrown and decayed and access to the underground areas requires special permission.

Fort du Salbert to Châlonvillars,
4.5km (3 miles), 1hr 15min
Restaurant in Châlonvillars.

Cross the top of the fort, and take the steps to the lower level. Follow the path past the entrance gates to a large grassy area with the ruins of a signalling tower in the centre. Continue to the road and branch right, onto a footpath almost opposite the car park, dropping down to join the road at a hairpin. Take the track leaving to the right off the bend. This soon passes a sign to a viewpoint with a small shelter.

Back on the track the route continues down through dense woods. After crossing a track, it curves left and follows along the top of a raised embankment, once part of a railway that supplied the military. Further on are the overgrown remains of another old military site.

Keep to this track for about half an hour, emerging from the woods and continuing through farmland until **Châlonvillars** comes into view. When the track meets a minor road, follow this over the canal bridge, cross the N19 and go down the D218 opposite, leading to the village square.

Fort du Salbert signalling tower

Châlonvillars to Échenans-sous-Mont-Vaudois, 6km (3.5 miles), 2hr

Go to the right at the *lavoir* (washing area) taking a lane which climbs steeply and joins a road by the church. Turn right and follow the road out of the village. As the houses are left behind, the views open up over Belfort. Continue into woods along this track for about 10min to a fork. Stay on the lower path, and very soon this arrives at a spring and marker stone.

Turn left at a junction, where paths right and ahead are less distinct, and carry on to the D218. Turn right for several hundred metres, and after a right-hand bend, turn left along a substantial track towards Échenans-sous-Mont-Vaudois.

The cross, which is reached within a few minutes, marks the place where a mother and her daughters were killed by lightning in 1792.

After 5min look out for a junction where the GR5 turns along a narrower track to the right, heading towards the Croix des Femmes. ◀ Shortly afterwards the route follows the main track when it swings 90 degrees to the left (ignore other minor tracks).

There follows a stretch of at least 1km along this vehicle track before it emerges onto a road with a village in sight to the left. Turn left into **Échenans-sous-Mont-Vaudois**. There is no shop or café, but drinking water is available on the road out of the village (see below). On reaching a T-junction turn left, then right, along Rue du Levant.

Échenans-sous-Mont-Vaudois to Brévilliers, 3.5km (2 miles), 1hr
Hotel, restaurants, cafés and shops in Héricourt (3km off-route).

This road leads out of the village to a turning circle, passing (at time of writing) a drinking water tap, then continues as a track. Follow this between woods, and where it turns left the route leaves to the right along a gravel track. Within about 5min this arrives at a junction where the path to the right is signed to Héricourt, but the GR5 carries straight on.

Fork right to reach the edge of the woods, then cross a large field in sight of a busy road. Take the bridge over this dual carriageway to pass the first few houses of **Brévilliers**. Cross the N83 and go up Rue de la Barrière opposite, then continue to the village square.

CLOCHER COMTOIS

The curved dome of the church belltower in Brévilliers is an indication that the route has now passed into Franche-Comté. This region, which extends from Belfort down to the Jura, has a distinctive style of belltower often called a *clocher comtois*. The graceful domes on these towers are sometimes decorated with coloured tiles to form geometric patterns. There are over 650 clochers comtois within Franche-Comté, and several can be found near the route of the GR5, with colourful examples at Héricourt, Les Fourgs and Pontarlier.

Turn right if you wish to leave the GR5 to go to **Héricourt**, where there is a railway station and other facilities (station 2km, town centre 3km).

From Brévilliers to Héricourt

To reach Héricourt turn right at the lavoir and fork left along Rue des Chalets. Carry on out of the village, then turn right, onto a side track, and follow yellow triangle waymarks through an access gap. Cross the meadow, going over a footbridge and into the woods. Keep on this yellow triangle route, which soon turns left downhill to the edge of Héricourt.

SECTION 8
GR5 BRÉVILLIERS TO ST-HIPPOLYTE

Beyond Brévilliers

SECTION SUMMARY TABLE

Start	Distance	Ascent/Descent	Time
Brévilliers	6.5km (4 miles)	50m/70m	1hr 45min
Châtenois-les-Forges	2.5km (1.5 miles)	0m/0m	45min
Nommay	6km (3.5 miles)	0m/0m	1hr 35min
Fesches-le-Châtel	6.5km (4 miles)	60m/50m	2hr
Dasle	1.5km (1 mile)	50m/0m	30min
Vandoncourt	4.5km (3 miles)	190m/10m	1hr 30min
Abbévillers	10km (6 miles)	280m/260m	3hr
Villars-lès-Blamont	5.5km (3.5 miles)	210m/140m	1hr 45min
Chamesol	4km (2.5 miles)	20m/250m	1hr

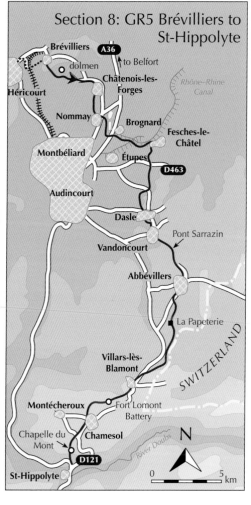

Section 8: GR5 Brévilliers to St-Hippolyte

The Montbéliard region is one of the more heavily populated parts of France, with a concentration of industrial towns, but the GR5 is skilfully routed through woodland and small villages.

The initial part of the route crosses the lowlands of the Belfort Gap, with few significant gradients – indeed, many parts are practically flat. Just outside Nommay it passes two large lakes with a leisure centre and then continues through the countryside using canal towpaths and quiet rural tracks, where in early summer there is a good chance of hearing nightingales. The landscape varies as the path crosses onto limestone country, passing an impressive natural rock arch at Pont Sarrazin. The route then rises to run beside the Swiss frontier, where border marker stones become common features along the way.

Approaching Dasle

Finally, the GR5 descends to the hillside chapel of Chapelle du Mont, where the view over St-Hippolyte is revealed. The town lies enclosed in the valley of the Doubs, overlooked on all sides by wooded hills.

This section can be walked in two days, but since it may be necessary to drop off-route for accommodation, three days may be required. There is a hotel in Étupes, and accommodation in Montbéliard or Audincourt, which can be reached by bus from Hérimoncourt (2km off-route from Abbévillers).

SECTION 8

Brévilliers to St-Hippolyte

Start	Brévilliers
Distance	47km (29 miles)
Maps	IGN TOP100 sheets 122 and 137

From Héricourt to Brévilliers

This section of the GR5 starts from the village of Brévilliers, accessible from Héricourt railway station by a 2km route waymarked with yellow triangles. Turn right from the railway station and then right across a level crossing. Follow the vehicle track uphill. After about half a kilometre turn right onto a smaller track which becomes a footpath. In less than 5min turn right at a T-junction. Keep to the path through meadowland and across a footbridge. Carry on almost to the corner of the field and leave by an access gap onto a narrow track. Turn right, then left at a T-junction to reach Brévilliers.

Brévilliers to Châtenois-les-Forges, 6.5km (4 miles), 1hr 45min

Hotel, restaurants, cafés and shops in Héricourt (3km off-route); restaurant, café and shops in Châtenois-les-Forges.

From the centre of **Brévilliers** go uphill to the right of the church. Turn left up a pedestrian way between houses then right along Rue de la Chevrette. Turn left up Rue du Vô and curve round to the left, where it becomes a quiet road between fields. Fork right at the next junction, where the left fork leads to a **dolmen** about 1km off-route, which has been excavated and is protected by a shelter.

The road winds through fields and copses, rising to a ridge. Drop down and carry on along the woodland edge to enter the woods ahead. After a few minutes take a broad footpath left, towards Nommay.

For the next few minutes the path passes some stones with worn markings. These are the historic **border markers** of the Principality of Montbéliard, which was a separate entity until the end of the 18th century.

The track swings right, and becomes more defined, with broad verges. Follow this track beneath a railway and on until it meets a road coming in from the left. Carry straight on into **Châtenois-les-Forges** along Rue du Maréchal Foch.

At a roundabout, bright with bedding plants in season, the village shops are straight on, but the GR5 takes Rue Kléber, to the right. Turn left into Rue de Villars, and right at a corner by a sandstone cross, to leave the village by Rue de Lieutenant Bidaux.

Châtenois-les-Forges to Nommay, 2.5km (1.5 miles), 45min

When this road turns sharply left, the route carries straight on between fields. Enter **Nommay** and follow Rue du Cimetière down to the N437. Go over to Rue des Jardins and follow this street until it comes out onto the D424. Turn right and cross the bridge over the River Savoureuse, and immediately beyond, turn right along a lane into a nature reserve.

Curve to the right, then take a path along a raised bank on the right, passing between the river and a lake. Keep straight ahead to pass beside a second lake – there is a leisure centre on the far bank. The GR5 curves round the beach at the end then climbs some steps leading over a footbridge to a car park. Turn left and head up to a bridge over the A36.

Nommay to Fesches-le-Châtel, 6km (3.5 miles), 1hr 35min
Hotel in Étupes (3km off-route); restaurants, cafés and shops in Fesches-le-Châtel (2km off-route).

The canal near Brognard

Cross the bridge. **Brognard** is immediately ahead, but the route turns right, down to the tree-lined canal towpath. On reaching a basin where two canal spurs meet, follow the towpath across an aqueduct spanning a river. Turn left over a small bridge, then right for a few hundred metres. Cross another bridge and turn left along the towpath (or turn right for accommodation in Étupes) then walk towards Fesches-le-Châtel.

After about 1km there is a road bridge. Leave the canal and turn right, along Rue du Canal, into **Fesches-le-Châtel**. Turn right at a church. A left turn would reach the village centre, but the facilities are 2km away.

Fesches-le-Châtel to Dasle, 6.5km (4 miles), 2hr
Restaurant and shop in Dasle.

Turn left up Rue de l'Égalité and fork left to pass the cemetery. Follow the track right, to enter woods by an open shelter, then turn left up a lane and cross the D463. Fork right on a lesser path, and some distance later, the route turns sharply left, then at a small clearing turns right to follow a winding footpath through the woods.

Cross over a road to a small but clearly marked footpath, which curves right to run parallel with an embankment. At a broad forestry track a GR cross blocks the path on the opposite side. Turn left towards the Forêt Communale d'Exincourt, but immediately look out for waymarks on a footpath forking to the left. Follow this path for a little over 1km until the GR5 turns sharply left and continues just inside the forest edge before coming out between two fields. **Dasle** is just ahead.

Turn left towards the cemetery and carry on into the village. Turn right at the old village water trough (to reach the village shop, turn left then right). Go left at the war memorial and curve round to reach the D126, turn left and very soon right into Rue des Aiguillottes.

Dasle to Vandoncourt, 1.5km (1 mile), 30min
Restaurant and shop in Vandoncourt.

This road passes between plots with fruit trees, then heads to the right of a depot with storage tanks. The road ends, but a vehicle track carries on, rising towards a ridge. Where the track turns left, follow it to come out between hedges. Turn left along the road past a cemetery, with the rooftops of **Vandoncourt** ahead. At Rue du Piquet turn right, into the village.

Vandoncourt to Abbévillers, 4.5km (3 miles), 1hr 30min
Bakery in Abbévillers.

Pass the village shop, cross the D253 and go down Rue des Damas. Follow signs to Pont Sarrazin, along Rue du Pont Sarrazin, then fork right. The road ends at the creeper-clad restaurant, La Cachette. Here, take the rough track alongside.

Climb some steps through the woods and follow the side of a small gorge, to in front of **Pont Sarrazin**. This impressive arch links the sides of the gorge to form a natural bridge.

Turn right and climb a footpath zigzagging to the lip of the gorge. Follow the main path left. ◄ At a T-junction,

A small path branches off left onto the bridge itself, but this is not part of the route.

THE LEGEND OF PONT SARRAZIN

The rock arch at Pont Sarrazin

There are several versions of this legend. According to one, a local maiden was carried off by a marauding Saracen. Rather than allow herself to be captured, she threw herself from his horse into the ravine, but her fall was stopped by the miraculous appearance of this bridge of rock. When her abductor tried to follow on horseback, the bridge was too narrow and he fell to his death. There is also a more prosaic explanation for the origin of the arch, involving the erosion of limestone by water trickling through the rock.

turn right and follow this track through thinning woodland. At the end of the woods it snakes on through fields, becoming a lane.

On emerging onto a side road, turn left, then almost immediately right, down the road heading towards **Abbévillers**. At the main street, take Rue de la Doué, almost opposite.

Abbévillers to Villars-lès-Blamont, 10km (6 miles), 3hr
Restaurant in La Papeterie.

Towards the edge of Abbévillers, turn left up a lane through fields and back into woods, gradually descending into a small gorge to reach a stream. Cross by a footbridge and turn right, along the bank.

Join a track and continue straight on to a junction, then turn right, currently signed to La Papeterie. A small river soon flows alongside and some buildings come into sight beyond the riverside fields. The GR5 takes a track to the left, which crosses the river and curves towards these buildings. Just beside the restaurant of **La Papeterie**, the GR5 takes a stony track to the left and climbs through a fern-filled gorge.

Almost at the top of the slope, turn right, along a woodland path roughly following the border with Switzerland – there are border stones along the next stretch of the route. Climb some steps to the left and follow the path ahead.

> The **border stones** beside this section of the path have an 'F' on the French side, and a shield with a bear – for the Canton of Bern – or a Swiss cross on the Swiss side. Many of them are dated 1817. After many years of turmoil in Europe, Napoleon was finally defeated and France was forced to agree to give up all territorial gains. These issues were all discussed at the Congress of Vienna in 1815 and many central European boundaries were rationalised as a result.

Cross a vehicle track and, still following border stones, continue between woods and pasture, passing a picnic table among trees. At a fork twist sharply left, then take the path that hairpins up a steep bank ahead. Continue, then leave the woods at a metal stile. Cross a pasture, and look out for another yellow metal stile to the left, then turn right, along a vehicle track. ◄ As the track becomes a lane, follow this downhill, then turn left as indicated into **Villars-lès-Blamont**. Fork left, pass the church and continue to the D73.

To the right, a series of small villages are spread across the landscape towards Montbéliard in the distance.

Villars-lès-Blamont to Chamesol,
5.5km (3.5 miles), 1hr 45min
Restaurant in Chamesol.

Cross this road and take Rue du Lomont uphill, by an ironwork cross. Pass a lane to a house on the right, then very soon after look out for a narrow footpath with a way-mark into woods to the right.

In a few minutes the route meets a road and follows it uphill. At a hairpin to the left, the GR5 leaves, carrying on roughly straight ahead. Follow the waymarks, taking the uphill track into woods.

The path contours along the side of a hill, negotiates a small rocky cleft, then climbs quite steeply. This arrives at a deep, rock-cut ditch with ramparts above which form part of the **Fort Lomont Battery**. Follow the signs to the viewpoint on the top of the battery. ▶ From the viewpoint, the route continues past some dilapidated fortifications, recrosses the ditch, then drops gradually to a path junction.

The platform gave a commanding position for artillery, with munitions being stored in the galleries beneath.

Go downhill, and along the side of a pasture to reach a track. Turn right at a lane, and follow this round to the left where a farm entrance (Ferme du Lomont) lies ahead. Leave to the left along a vehicle track, heading towards the farm of Le Tremblais, but before reaching it, just beyond a large metal tank, follow waymarks to the right. This short path reaches a road. Turn right to **Chamesol** and continue downhill at the first house. At a T-junction turn right, then left just before the restaurant, À Mon Plaisir.

Chamesol to St-Hippolyte, 4km (2.5 miles), 1hr
Hotels, campsite, restaurants, cafés and
shops in St-Hippolyte (just off-route).

Follow this quiet road and cross the D121 to take a foot-path opposite, through fields, and enter woodland again. The path goes down the side of a wooded gorge, twisting around hairpins at a steep section. Where it meets a lane, the route goes downhill.

St-Hippolyte

Further down is a signpost left to **Chapelle du Mont**, where there is view over St-Hippolyte. Take a stony footpath from the front of the clearing going down in a series of zigzags to the road.

Turn left, then cross the D121 and walk down beside a cemetery to reach the D121 again. Continue downhill to a junction, where the GR5 turns left, but carrying straight on gives access to **St-Hippolyte** with its range of facilities.

SECTION 9
GR5 ST-HIPPOLYTE TO VILLERS-LE-LAC

The valley of the Doubs

This section of the walk is quite unlike any of the others, as much of the way follows the limestone gorge cut by the River Doubs.

Starting above St-Hippolyte, a town that sits low down in the Doubs Valley, the GR5 follows the river to Soulce-Cernay. It then shortcuts over higher ground before rejoining the river at the village of Goumois.

Beyond Goumois the route follows the Doubs and includes some spectacular stretches of river gorge. While in places the sides of the valley slope gently down to the quiet river below, along other stretches the river has produced a deep, narrow pathway between cliffs.

A couple of centuries ago all sorts of industries were drawn into the area to make use of the power of the river. Today these workshops are gone. One of the attractions of the path through the gorge is that this is isolated country, long stretches of the route being without sign of habitation.

Towards the end of the section the Saut du Doubs waterfall, seen at its best after heavy rains, is a popular destination for riverboat cruises from Villers-le-Lac. Other points of interest include the little chapel at Urtière, with traditional

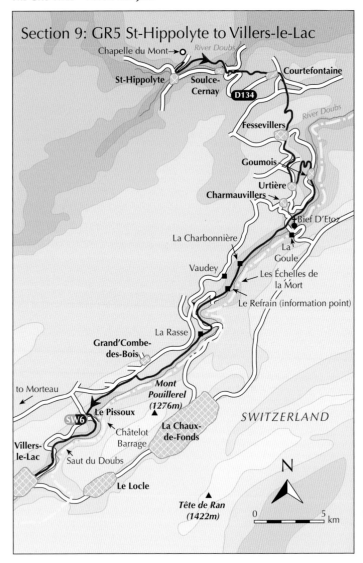

Section 9: GR5 St-Hippolyte to Villers-le-Lac

Chapelle du Mont
River Doubs
St-Hippolyte
Soulce-Cernay
Courtefontaine
D134
River Doubs
Fessevillers
Goumois
Urtière
Charmauvillers
Bief D'Etoz
La Charbonnière
La Goule
Vaudey
Les Échelles de la Mort
Le Refrain (information point)
La Rasse
Grand'Combe-des-Bois
Mont Pouillerel (1276m)
SWITZERLAND
to Morteau
SW6
Le Pissoux
Châtelot Barrage
La Chaux-de-Fonds
Villers-le-Lac
Saut du Doubs
Le Locle
Tête de Ran (1422m)
N
0   5 km

tavaillons (wooden shingles) cladding the belltower, and the excellent information display at Le Refrain.

This section can be walked in three days, with suggested stops at Goumois and either the hotel at La Rasse or off-route at Biaufond in Switzerland. Lack of public transport makes leaving the route at Villers-le-Lac difficult. A taxi to Morteau is possible, otherwise walk on to leave the route at Pontarlier.

SECTION SUMMARY TABLE			
Start	Distance	Ascent/Descent	Time
St-Hippolyte	4km (2.5 miles)	60m/120m	1hr 15min
Soulce-Cernay	5.5km (3.5 miles)	420m/20m	1hr 45min
Courtefontaine	7.5km (4.5 miles)	190m/130m	2hr 15min
Fessevillers	7km (4.5 miles)	140m/490m	2hr 15min
Goumois	5.5km (3.5 miles)	20m/0m	1hr 45min
Bief d'Etoz	5km (3 miles)	70m/0m	1hr 30min
La Charbonnière	3km (2 miles)	0m/80m	1hr
Le Refrain	7km (4.5 miles)	40m/20m	2hr 15min
La Rasse	16km (10 miles)	370m/280m	4hr 45min
Châtelot Barrage	3.5km (2 miles)	10m/0m	1hr
Saut du Doubs	7km (4.5 miles)	150m/120m	2hr

SECTION 9

St-Hippolyte to Villers-le-Lac

Start	St-Hippolyte
Distance	71km (44 miles)
Maps	IGN TOP100 sheet 137

Note: If wild camping, be aware of warnings about water-level fluctuations.

St-Hippolyte to Soulce-Cernay, 4km (2.5 miles), 1hr 15min

Hotels, campsite, restaurants, cafés and shops in St-Hippolyte (just off-route).

Turn into Rue de la Baumotte, then immediately left up some steps to join a footpath which contours above the road. Continue in this direction until reaching a T-junction, and turn right. Look out for a junction just beyond a large old farm building, where the signpost indicates a sharp right turn, downhill, but the path is hard to see. Go down the field to find an obvious path, which becomes a little sunken track descending beside a stream.

A sign, the first of many, warns that water levels can rise suddenly because of dams and power plants upstream.

After crossing a small bridge below a waterfall, the route turns right, passing a chalet, then continues downhill beside the stream. The track becomes a road, then joins another small road at La Saunerie. Continue straight on, with the tree-lined banks of the **River Doubs** off to the right. ◀

The **River Doubs** will become familiar over the course of the next few days. Rising on the Jura plateau close to Mouthe, it has a particularly convoluted course. While the straight-line distance between the source and end of the river is

Soulce-Cernay

only 90km, the river flows for 453km to achieve this. From Mouthe, where the Doubs emerges from a cave as a sizeable stream, it flows north-east, defining the Franco-Swiss border for many kilometres. There follows a huge meander into Switzerland before the river turns back, finally flowing into the Saône.

Cross the road bridge over the Doubs. To the right lies the small village of **Soulce-Cernay**.

**Soulce-Cernay to Courtefontaine,
5.5km (3.5 miles), 1hr 45min**
Bar/restaurant in Courtefontaine.

Turn left from the bridge then immediately right, up a minor road. Where this ends, scramble up the bank by the buried storage tank onto a track which then climbs to join the D134. Turn left, and look out for a footpath leaving on the left.

Only a few minutes later the path skirts pasture, then carries on uphill through more woodland to rejoin the D134. Turn left, but then leave to the left, down a foot-path into woods.

The view opens out, with a line of limestone outcrops marking the upper levels of the Doubs Valley.

The path joins a lane that comes up from the right. Continue straight on, and after a steep uphill section the route emerges close to the farm of La Joux. Go around the front of the building, then follow the vehicle track across pasture. ◄

The track swings around a second small farm building, La Rasse, and becomes a lane, continuing uphill for over a kilometre to reach **Courtefontaine**. At a crossroads go straight on along Rue du Lavoir.

LAVOIRS

Like many villages in the north of Franche-Comté, Courtefontaine has an imposing *lavoir* (washing area). A miniature Greek temple may seem an over-the-top way of embellishing the local water supply, but a reliable source of water was something to be valued in a limestone landscape where surface water can be scarce. These ornate lavoirs date from the late 18th and early 19th centuries, a time of relative rural prosperity. The buildings contained the water source (*fontaine*) that supplied the lavoir, and usually a nearby animal drinking trough (*abreuvoir*). Long since out of use, some have been demolished, but others are valued as a link with the past.

Close to the farm of La Joux

**Courtefontaine to Fessevillers,
7.5km (4.5 miles), 2hr 15min**
Gîte in Fessevillers.

*Entering
Courtefontaine*

Cross the road by the colonnaded lavoir and go straight
ahead, along the road beside the war memorial.

Turn left at a T-junction, and follow this quiet road
for about 0.5km to the D134, turn right, passing Rue
les Vareilles, and look out for a gateway on the right
where the GR5 leaves. Although there is no obvious path
beyond, the route heads across the field, first passing a
waymark on a powerline post, then making for an access
on the far side. Head across the next field towards the
road junction beyond.

Once out of the field take the road opposite, signposted for La Mine, passing a farm and reaching some
farm buildings, where the GR5 follows the road as it turns
right. Follow this lane for the next 2km, passing the house
of Le Creux. The tarmac ends beside an isolated farm.
Carry on along the track ahead.

After only about 200 metres, look out for a tricky
change of direction. The route leaves on a faint vehicle
track across the field to the left, and is indicated by a
waymark on the right, but this is half hidden. If you miss

this, there is also a cross on a tree ahead. Follow the faint track across the field and through a gate, then across the next field, entering a small copse. The path emerges onto a lane in front of the farm of Montsassier-dessous.

Turn right and follow this lane for about 1km until it hairpins left, then leave by a grassy path rising on the right, which curves away to join a vehicle track.

The route leads on through pasture and woodland and at a fork, stays with the right-hand, waymarked track. Where this track turns sharply right, the GR5 leaves by a footpath to the left. Cross a tiny stream then climb some steps, turn right, towards the church, then left, past the gîte d'étape, to reach the main road in **Fessevillers**.

Fessevillers to Goumois, 7km (4.5 miles), 2hr 15min
Hotel, campsite, café/restaurants and shop in Goumois.

Turn right, along the road, then left up Rue d'Urtière. Climb out of the village, turning right at the junction where Rue de la Fromagerie leaves to the left, then follow left to pass in front of a farm. After about 0.5km, take the road to the left towards Mont-de-Fessevillers.

Continue along this road for another kilometre as far as the farm at Sur-le-Mont. Soon after, where the road bends sharply right, go down the track that carries on ahead. Turn right at a road and continue for about 2km, passing the buildings of **Urtière**, and turning left at a small chapel just beyond.

On reaching a lane, turn left, towards Goumois. At the next junction, turn right, and carry on past the turn off to **Charmauvillers** until the route is directed off to the left, leaving by farm buildings. Drop down onto a footpath and continue down through woods for about 20min to reach a lane and turn left.

The lane hairpins right, then after a few hundred metres, turn left following a waymarked track towards Goumois, and continue downhill to the D437. Turn right, then left down a minor road opposite the Hotel Taillard, and follow downhill to the centre of **Goumois** (the camp-site is about 1km north).

Goumois to Bief d'Etoz, 5.5km (3.5 miles), 1hr 45min
Restaurant (La Goule, Switzerland) by Bief d'Etoz.

Turn right, and follow the main road out of the village. Just beyond the last houses, a *sentier d'interprétation* (interpretive trail) to the left is also the GR5, and it soon emerges onto a minor road.

Turn left along the valley, with the River Doubs away to the left. The road ends at a picnic area and the GR5 continues along a track. Stay with this major footpath, which keeps low down by the river.

A few minutes later some buildings come into sight on the Swiss bank. The main path drops down towards the river, but waymarks point off to the right along a narrower path through the woods. This leads over a short rocky section, then drops back closer to river level. ▸

A higher-level alternative is signed to the right for use if there is flooding.

Keep with this riverside path, following waymarks, and using a short fixed ladder at one point. Soon afterwards the path reaches a hut accessed by a vehicle track. Join the track and continue along the valley. A hydroelectric generating station comes into view on the Swiss bank, and a few minutes later the path passes the little chapel of Bief d'Etoz and joins a road.

The River Doubs at La Goule

Bief d'Ftoz to La Charbonnière, 5km (3 miles), 1hr 30min
Shelter in La Charbonnière.

The GR5 continues along the road, but where this hairpins left, the GR carries straight on. To access the restaurant **La Goule**, just off-route, keep on the road and cross onto the Swiss side of the river.

Approximately 25min after leaving the road by La Goule, the GR5 takes a footpath to the left. This leads past La Verrerie du Bief d'Etoz, the site of a long-abandoned glass-making workshop. The scant remains are hidden in the vegetation, but there is an information board. Carry straight on. The path rises from the banks of the Doubs to join a track. Continue uphill, then fork left, as signed to Charbonnière du Haut. This joins a lane just before **La Charbonnière**, an old farm now converted into a shelter.

La Charbonnière to Le Refrain, 3km (2 miles), 1hr
Hotel in Bois de la Biche (1.5km off-route);
shelter (old chapel) in Le Refrain.

There are two possible routes from here. The main GR5 route branches down towards the river just before the shelter and is signposted 'GR5 Le Refrain par le bord du Doubs'. This keeps closely to the riverbank all the way to **Le Refrain**, where the little shelter on the far side of the car park has benches, and a wealth of information relating to the locality. The alternative route is at a higher level and rejoins the main route at Le Refrain.

The alternative route is worth considering, as it includes the descent of **Les Échelles de la Mort**, three long, fixed metal ladders. They are sturdily built and have hand-rails, so climbing down can be done reasonably safely. This route also gives access to the refuge of **Vaudey** (currently closed). To follow this alternative, carry on along the vehicle track past the shelter, following the sign to GR5 Le Refrain par Les Échelles de la Mort. It passes an open lookout point above the gorge, just before reaching the top of the ladders. At the bottom, a clear path leads onto the car park at Le Refrain.

The **Refrain Hydroelectric Plant** is now totally automatic; there have been no permanent staff on site since 1980. Prior to that, for many years there was an isolated community living here in the gorge. Men working in the plant would bring their wives and families. The children attended a school on site, which in its heyday had up to 20 pupils – the school closed in 1971. The little chapel, which dates back to these times, is now used as a shelter.

Le Refrain to La Rasse, 7km (4.5 miles), 2hr 15min
Gîte in Biaufond (0.5km off-route);
hotel/restaurant in La Rasse.

Leave the car park along the access road, and follow waymarks through woods to the left to reach the dam at Barrage du Refrain. Pass the dam, then a barrier, and continue along the stony footpath close to the waterside, to reach a metal ladder taking the path to a higher level.

The route gradually drops back to river level, and passes the ruins of the old farm of Gaillots. A little way beyond, the track curves off to the right and the GR5 takes a footpath down through trees on the left. This emerges close to a parking area where waymarks point up some steps to the D464. ▶

For accommodation at Biaufond, leave the route here and cross into Switzerland.

Cross the road and take the footpath up into woods. The river takes a sweeping turn here and the path drops down to rejoin the riverbank beyond. Continue for a further kilometre to reach the hotel/restaurant at **La Rasse**.

La Rasse to Châtelot Barrage, 16km (10 miles), 4hr 45min
Shelter in Abri du Torret.

After about a half an hour, pass the old glass-working site of La Verrerie de la Guêpe, which had a furnace until 1820. Beyond this, 3km from La Rasse, is a signposted path junction. The GR5 carries on to the left, soon passing Kiosque Bonaparte, then an unlocked fishing hut. Another hydroelectric station comes into view on the Swiss bank. ▶

The gorge is particularly steep sided here and the power station incorporates a funicular for access.

The old GR5 route through the gorge ahead is no longer recommended, owing to the danger of rock falls, so the current route diverts to a higher level at the Abri du Torret, another accessible shelter. Leave to the right by the Sentier du Moulin, and after passing beneath some powerlines carry straight ahead at two junctions (signed towards Villebasse), and continue to climb. At the top of the forest, turn left, head for the left-hand corner of the first field, then cross the next field to the D211. Turn left and as the road enters forest, fork left towards the farm of Les Planots, but then carry straight on along a forest track.

Just past the tiny Cabane des Douaniers, fork left downhill. At a large farm building, leave the track and carry straight on. Turn right at Gourdavi junction, and keep on this track until the first houses of **Le Pissoux** come into view, then take a rough track down to the left. Where this curves right near a small cave of overhanging limestone slabs, take a footpath to the right. From the next junction, follow signs to the **Châtelot Barrage** car park.

The falls at Saut du Doubs

Châtelot Barrage to Saut du Doubs, 3.5km (2 miles), 1hr
Café, restaurant and snack stalls at Saut du Doubs.

Take the path down from the car park towards the dam, passing a viewpoint overlooking the gorge. Continue down a flight of steps then follow a broad path towards Saut du Doubs climbing up from the river.

Fork left down a narrower footpath which in turn leads to a gravel path. Follow this downhill, and continue along the side of Lac Moron. This level track reaches a rather striking feature where the river runs between two opposite rocky headlands, and the route passes beneath a rock arch. Beyond, the path climbs through woods. Continue upwards as the sound of a waterfall grows louder, to reach the viewing area of the **Saut du Doubs** falls.

Saut du Doubs to Villers-le-Lac, 7km (4.5 miles), 2hr
Gîte in Le Cerneux Billard (3km off-route); hotels, gîte, restaurants, cafés and shops in Villers-le-Lac.

Carry on down the concrete path, which leads towards the embarkation point for pleasure boats from Villers-le-Lac, passing some tourist kiosks and a café/restaurant. Take the road up to the right, pass a barrier, then climb a steep earth path up to the left. Turn left on emerging onto a road, then climb some steps on the right, and continue to the sign at Les Vions. (Leave here for the gîte at Cerneux Billard.) Be aware that GR waymarks lead off in both directions. For the main GR5 route, turn left down the road for a few metres, then right, down a lane with a 'no entry' sign. ▶

An alternative route to Les Alliés leaves by following waymarks ahead through the car park.

Following the main route, this quiet road becomes Route des Combes. Continue straight on at the next junction. Follow the road alongside the river into **Villers-le-Lac** to reach a main road in the town centre.

SECTION 10
GR5 VILLERS-LE-LAC TO LES HÔPITAUX-NEUFS

Near Les Seignes

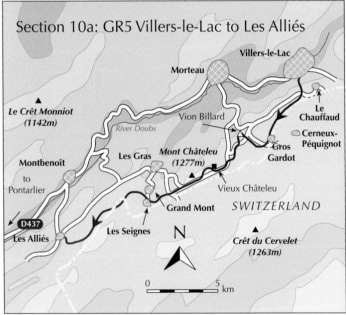

Section 10a: GR5 Villers-le-Lac to Les Alliés

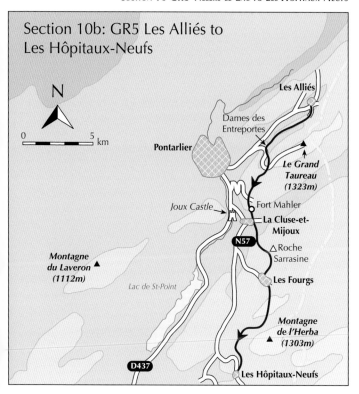

Section 10b: GR5 Les Alliés to Les Hôpitaux-Neufs

This section leads across the open landscape of the Jura, where villages are sparse and isolated. There are several panoramic viewpoints along the way, including the striking outlook over Joux Castle in its eagle's-nest setting.

From Villers-le-Lac the GR5 rejoins the Swiss border after a long, steady climb. The landscape, and particularly the buildings, become noticeably more Alpine, and a series of vertical limestone rocks, the Dames des Entreportes, form an unusual geological feature beside the route. The path then climbs to reach Fort Mahler, a mid19th-century fort overlooking the narrow valley of La Cluse-et-Mijoux. From the lookout point on the end of the promontory, Joux Castle on its massive limestone outcrop is suddenly revealed – the castle is ideally sited to defend the narrow gorge below.

Beyond Joux, the route passes the viewpoint at Roche Sarrasine, before reaching Les Fourgs and the winter sports area of Métabief.

Currently, the accommodation on this section is not evenly spaced. The choice is between four short days, with suggested stops at Les Seignes, Les Alliés, and Les Fourgs, or three days, stopping at Les Seignes, then a long day to off-route accommodation in Pontarlier.

Public transport in this area is somewhat restricted, so be aware that there are currently no buses to Villers-le-Lac and buses linking with Les Hôpitaux-Neufs are infrequent.

SECTION SUMMARY TABLE			
Start	**Distance**	**Ascent/Descent**	**Time**
Villers-le-Lac	10km (6 miles)	540m/210m	3hr 15min
Gros Gardot	6.5km (4 miles)	240m/130m	2hr
Vieux Château	5km (3 miles)	40m/170m	1hr 30min
Les Seignes	9km (5.5 miles)	130m/240m	2hr 45min
Les Alliés	5.5km (3.5 miles)	40m/120m	1hr 45min
Dames des Entreportes	9km (5.5 miles)	210m/230m	2hr 45min
La Cluse-et-Mijoux	8km (5 miles)	210m/0m	2hr 30min
Les Fourgs	11km (7 miles)	50m/90m	3hr 15min

SECTION 10
Villers-le-Lac to Les Hôpitaux-Neufs

Start	Villers-le-Lac
Distance	64km (39.5 miles)
Maps	IGN TOP100 sheet 137

**Villers-le-Lac to Gros Gardot,
10km (6 miles), 3hr 15min**
*Hotels, gîte, restaurants, cafés and shops in
Villers-le-Lac; auberge/gîte in Sur la Roche.*

Cross the bridge from the centre of **Villers-le-Lac**, turn
right along Rue de la Gare, then left up Rue du Stade. Go
through a small park, and turn left to a main road. Turn
right, and right again almost immediately under a large
road bridge, then take a minor road to the left. As this
snakes uphill, the view back over Villers-le-Lac opens out.

The road leads across a level crossing, then bends
sharply left, and the GR5 leaves by a track to the right,

FARMSTEADS OF THE JURA

The farmsteads of the Jura have shallow-pitched overhanging roofs similar
to those of their Alpine neighbours. In winter these roofs ensure that rain
and snow are carried well away from the base of the walls. Traditionally,
the walls are further protected by wooden shingles known as *tavaillons*. In
summer, water collected from this large roof area can be a useful resource,
as there are few sources of surface water in limestone country.

In response to the extreme cold and deep snow of winter, all the farm
buildings – house, barn and byre – are gathered under one roof. This gives
the house the advantages of the heat generated by the livestock. It also
means there is no need to go through deep snow to attend to the animals.

The *tuyé*, a huge chimney, is used not just for heat but also for smoking
meats and cheeses, with an adjustable cap that allows the smoking process
to be regulated.

towards **Le Chauffaud**. Keep to the main track uphill. The path enters a pasture bordered by forest, with Alpine-style houses on the slopes.

Further up the hill turn right, onto a lane that joins the road at the small settlement of Le Prélot. Turn right, but almost immediately leave by a track to the right towards Le Pralot. This track crosses pastureland, still climbing, with a large old farm coming into sight to the left. On reaching a lane, turn left, and follow this round in front of the farm of Gradoz Dessus, and on between pastures, then look out for waymarks pointing right.

Take the indistinct path going up the edge of a field to enter woods, and follow this to reach a fence at the top of the hill. Go into the pasture and turn left, following the edge of the forest, then turn right, downhill, to join a lane at the auberge/gîte of Sur la Roche. Follow this to the right, then turn right, along the D447.

Very soon leave the road through a small gate to the left. There is a faint vehicle track across this field and occasional waymarks on isolated trees. Head for a track that enters the woods by a stile, slightly to the left. Once into the woods join a track going steeply uphill. On reaching an old house with wooden cladding, turn right, taking a narrow, rocky path up towards the crest, beside a tumbled stone wall, to meet the Franco-Swiss border again.

The **border stones** here have chevrons on the Swiss side and fleurs-de-lis on the French side, and were erected in 1819. This is two years later than the date on the previous stones (Section 8) because of the particular history of the little village of Cerneux-Péquignot. Negotiations at the Congress of Vienna saw Switzerland laying claim to all the French territory east of the Doubs, but the French were unwilling to give up so much land and negotiated a compromise. It was finally agreed that only the commune of Cerneux-Péquignot would be ceded to the Swiss. This was against the wishes of the 300 inhabitants, and it was not until 1819, after much discussion, that the frontier stones were set up. Many people retained their French citizenship, but the village has remained a part of Switzerland ever since.

The route stays close to the ridge, passing a series of frontier stones and a ski-lift, and then begins to descend.

After crossing a pasture, join a lane at some farm buildings. The border stones follow a different line here, across fields to the left. Beyond, a view extends across the lush meadows and chalet rooftops of Switzerland. Follow the lane past some large farmsteads to the D48, and turn right. The tiny settlement of **Gros Gardot** lies just to the left.

Gros Gardot to Vieux Châteleu, 6.5km (4 miles), 2hr
Auberge/gîte in Vieux Châteleu.

Follow the road around a curve, then leave on the left just beyond a small wood along a track towards Les Feuves. When this reaches the farm, swing round farm buildings to a road. Turn left, then just by the auberge of Meix Lagor, take a woodland path to the right. Fork right, and continue to the D447.

Turn left, and leave on a footpath to the right, towards Vion Billard, the path follows a tumbledown wall up the hill. At the top of the field there is a stony footpath with signs to **Belvédère du Vion Billard** to the right, and the GR5 to the left. ▶

Back on the main footpath keep to the edge of a field, then head across the next field towards a large concrete cross. The path continues with an impressive cliff dropping down beyond the fence, fringed by trees.

In a few minutes the route reaches the D447 again. Turn right and at Les Cernoniers, leave on a track to the left which goes between a small chapel and an agricultural building into open woodland. A couple of minutes later follow a more minor track to the right, and where the route emerges onto the D447, turn left to reach the auberge at **Vieux Châteleu** in about half an hour.

The viewpoint is worth the detour to look out over the village of Derrière-le-Mont, set against a background of limestone outcrops and scattered farms.

Derrière-le-Mont

Vieux Châteleu to Les Seignes, 5km (3 miles), 1hr 30min
Chambres d'hôtes in Les Seignes.

Turn right off the road beyond the auberge, then go left up a stony vehicle track. Where the track forks, go left, but immediately look out for a small path dropping to the left, downhill through fields. Turn right along the bottom of the valley to join a woodland path.

About 5min later a footpath goes up to rejoin the D447. Turn right and follow the road downhill, with views of hills ranging into the distance. Pass a farm, Chez Voynot, and at the hamlet of Nid du Fol stay with the road when it turns sharply left.

On meeting the D404, turn right towards Les Gras, then leave to the left on a rough track. Carry on through a field, almost parallel to the road, and enter old conifer forest with tumbled boulders.

Towards Les Gras

The track continues along the forest edge, to reach the hamlet of **Les Seignes**, with the limestone edge of Rochers du Cerf beyond.

Les Seignes to Les Alliés, 9km (5.5km), 2hr 45min
Gîte in Les Alliés.

On reaching a road turn right, towards **Grand Mont** then left onto a broad vehicle track towards Le Théverot. Continue through fields, then woods, and watch out for a waymark to the right along a footpath. Turn right at a more significant track, and right again at a T-junction to reach the farm of Le Théverot.

Turn left, and continue uphill, eventually leaving the woodland. The route crosses pasture with a farm on the skyline ahead. A signpost points up the slope to the right, then, below the woods, another points left. Turn left through the farmyard at Côte du Cerf to join a track

153

which, once over the brow of the hill, descends through mixed woodland, curves round a clearing and returns into trees. Where the track swings round to the right and becomes a road, the GR5 leaves to the left. This leads through a rough clearing, approaching the hamlet of Cernet de Doubs.

Follow the route round the side of the first house, with a sign towards Les Alliés. This connects with a sunken track which hairpins down to a stream. Turn right, cross a footbridge, then cross back over on a concrete bridge, to continue down a broad track. The route stays beside the stream for about 20min as it descends into a small gorge, to emerge close to **Les Alliés**. The original name of Les Alliés was Les Allemands ('the Germans'), but the local people decided in 1915 that naming their village after 'the Allies' would be more appropriate.

Les Alliés to Dames des Entreportes, 5.5km (3.5 miles), 1hr 45min

Turn left out of **Les Alliés** then left again down a minor road towards La Barillette. Follow it as it rises through farmland dotted with large farmsteads and Alpine-style houses.

In front of the Ferme des Bonjours the GR5 turns left, still on the road towards La Barillette. Just before the next farmstead turn right, up a gravel track. At a set of direction boards, note that there are red and white GR waymarks to the left for the GTJ, but the GR5 goes up to the right, then veers right again down a grassy clearing. The way is not obvious: watch out for waymarks on isolated trees to reach a narrow path leading on through woods and crossing a small clearing.

A few hundred metres beyond, the GR5 follows the path round to the right, and joins a vehicle track going steeply downhill. Turn left on reaching a road to pass the Ferme des Moines.

At the next farm, the Ferme des Ouillettes, pass between the house and the barn then leave the road to the left. Follow round a bend, then take a lesser path to the left, uphill, to reach a track. Turn right, and continue downhill, staying with this track as it curves left to cross a bridge. Turn left along the road towards **Dames des Entreportes** where there is a striking jagged-edged vertical sheet of limestone.

Dames des Entreportes to La Cluse-et-Mijoux, 9km (5.5 miles), 2hr 45min
Campsite in Le Larmont (1.5km off-route); hotels, restaurants, cafés and shops in Pontarlier (3km off-route); restaurants, café/bar and bakery in La Cluse-et-Mijoux.

The GR5 takes Chemin du Morond opposite, and after passing Ferme de la Motte, this road crosses a small bridge. Follow a forest track to the left as it twists round and comes back up onto the road. Turn left, then within a couple of hundred metres, leave by a track to the right.

At a junction where the GTJ and the GR5 rejoin, carry straight on into a wide pasture, and follow the valley side. The track turns right, to reach a junction where the GR5 goes left (carry straight on for Le Larmont campsite near Pontarlier).

Joux Castle from Fer à Cheval

JOUX CASTLE

Joux Castle

The high point on which Joux Castle stands, overlooking the trade or invasion route of La Cluse-et-Mijoux, has been fortified for centuries. In the 11th century there was a wooden castle on the site, rebuilt in stone in the 12th and 13th centuries. Louis XIV's architect, Vauban, worked on Joux Castle in the 17th century, and Joffre (who later gained fame as a First World War commander) strengthened the defences in the 19th century. There are now five successive circling walls, the final one only being added after the Franco-Prussian War of 1870–71.

Despite its apparently impregnable position, the castle has changed hands many times. In 1480 it passed to Louis XI, as a result of bribery and betrayal. In 1507 it was captured by Austrians. In 1639 it was taken by Swedes, then offered by treaty to Spain. In 1668 Louis XIV took Joux unopposed, then it was returned by treaty to Spanish control, then retaken by France in 1674.

In the time of the revolution and the Napoleonic empire it became a state prison. A siege in 1814 saw the castle fall to invading Austrians, but negotiations at the Congress of Vienna restored French control.

The castle now contains a museum with a collection of weaponry.

At the next farm, Les Jantets, go through the farm-yard and continue to the road. Turn right, then soon left, down a cobbled, tree-lined track, following signs to Fort Mahler. ▸ There is no access to **Fort Mahler** itself, but a diversion round the edge of its rock-cut defensive ditch reveals a breathtaking view on the far side.The ground drops away steeply to the valley of La Cluse-et-Mijoux, with **Joux Castle** standing high on the promontory opposite.

Return to the entrance to Fort Mahler, and follow a grassy track down to **La Cluse-et-Mijoux**.

On the way, a sign indicates the lookout point at Belvédère du Fer à Cheval, less than 1km off-route, a worthwhile diversion, (leave here to go off-route to Pontarlier).

La Cluse-et-Mijoux to Les Fourgs,
8km (5 miles), 2hr 30min
Chambres d'hôtes, shops and restaurant in Les Fourgs.

Turn left along the D67 then right, down a road by a metal cross, and pass under the railway. Carry on uphill through open land, passing a little building to enter woodland. The path comes out at the small settlement of Montpetot, where the route continues up a track by a water trough. The path winds through woods, and on entering a large clearing, look out carefully for a waymark on a tree up to the left. This indicates a path which soon joins a track. Turn left and follow it through the woods, turning left at a farm building to reach the lookout point and small shelter at **Roche Sarrasine**.

Beyond the lookout, turn right and continue out onto the broad plateau, with Les Fourgs ahead. Turn right at a T-junction, then very soon afterwards, left into **Les Fourgs**.

Les Fourgs to Les Hôpitaux-Neufs,
11km (7 miles), 3hr 15min
Campsite, chambres d'hôtes, restaurants, café/bar and shops in Les Hôpitaux-Neufs.

Turn left along the main street then leave the road to climb to the hilltop chapel at Tourillot. Just beyond the chapel, turn right, along a track, and continue until reaching a

A sign points towards the Sapin Président, a huge old carved tree a few minutes off-route.

cattle grid. Look out for waymarks and leave to the left, to go around two sides of a field. Follow the waymarks beside a fence, over a low ridge with scattered trees, and join a track downhill through forest on the far side. Watch out for a path forking right, which reaches a picnic shelter where the GR leaves along a track to the right. ◄

The route continues past a large open shelter, then leaves by an access to the right, to follow alongside a low wall. At the Auberge du Vourbey turn right, up a track to go under powerlines. Leave at a signpost, going left, and crossing two fields. Follow the powerlines along a clearing to join a track, which becomes a lane, and reaches a road. Turn left, pass through the little settlement of La Beridole and at the next junction turn left for a very short distance.

Just after entering Hôpitaux-Vieux, turn left again to pass a small stadium. Follow the edge of the forest to skirt the village, eventually joining a road which crosses the N57. Beyond the bridge, turn sharply right to drop down into **Les Hôpitaux-Neufs**, then turn left towards the church.

SECTION 11
GR5 LES HÔPITAUX-NEUFS TO NYON

Near La Pile-Dessus

One of the real highlights of the whole walk is found in this section, the spectacular clifftop walk to the summit of Le Mont d'Or.

The route from Les Hôpitaux-Neufs climbs to the summit of Le Morond, then runs along the top of 200m-high limestone cliffs giving uninterrupted views over the Swiss Jura. The high point of Le Mont d'Or is just off-route, but easily reached by a short detour. The descent is by a gentler slope, passing the source of the River Doubs to reach the town of Mouthe.

From Mouthe as far as the Swiss border the route crosses the high plateau, much of which lies within the Haut-Jura regional park and is densely forested. Beyond Chapelle-des-Bois there is a very steep climb of about 250m to the look-out points of Roche Champion and Roche Bernard, which provide the best places on the route for an extended view over the Jura plateau. Two lakes lying just below the ridge, Lac de Bellefontaine and Lac des Mortes, add to the panorama.

From here the route makes its way to the small resort of Les Rousses, where the lively main street seems very tourist oriented compared with the more traditional villages nearby. Not far beyond, the GR5 passes close to the waterfall at Bief de la Chaille and then rises to reach the Swiss border. Beyond the village of St-Cergue the descent from the plateau begins, and the path drops rapidly down to flatter country by the shores of Lake Geneva, with a vista of the Alps beyond.

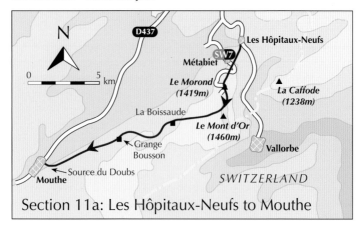

Section 11a: Les Hôpitaux-Neufs to Mouthe

This section does include some high and exposed walking. On the approach to Le Mont d'Or the path runs close to cliffs, which could present a hazard in poor visibility. It can be walked in four or five days, with suggested stops at Mouthe, Chapelle-des-Bois and Les Rousses.

SECTION SUMMARY TABLE			
Start	**Distance**	**Ascent/Descent**	**Time**
Les Hôpitaux-Neufs	4km (2.5 miles)	430m/0m	1hr 30min
Le Morond	5km (3 miles)	40m/240m	1hr 45min
La Boissaude	11.5km (7 miles)	0m/280m	3hr 30min
Mouthe	7.5km (4.5 miles)	60m/0m	2hr 15min
Chaux-Neuve	13.5km (8.5 miles)	250m/130m	4hr 15min
Chapelle-des-Bois	4.5km (3 miles)	210m/0m	2hr
Roche Bernard	7.5km (4.5 miles)	0m/70m	2hr 30min
Chalet Rose	7km (4 miles)	0m/120m	2hr
Les Rousses	6km (4 miles)	140m/100m	2hr
La Cure	8.5km (5.5 miles)	40m/140m	2hr 40min
St-Cergue	6.5km (4 miles)	0m/540m	2hr
Trélex	5km (3 miles)	0m/120m	1hr 30min

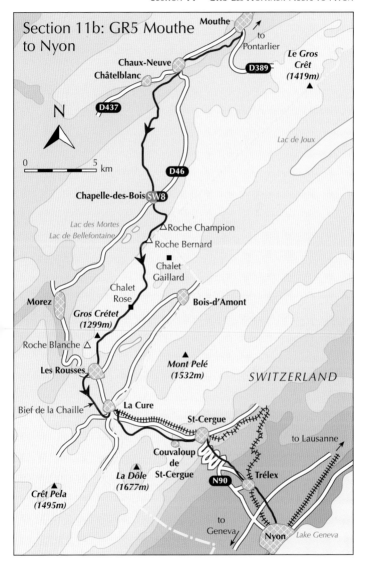

Section 11b: GR5 Mouthe to Nyon

Mouthe

to Pontarlier

D389

Le Gros Crêt (1419m)

Chaux-Neuve

Châtelblanc

D437

N

Lac de Joux

0   5 km

D46

Chapelle-des-Bois SW8

Lac des Mortes
Lac de Bellefontaine

△ Roche Champion

△ Roche Bernard

■ Chalet Gaillard

Chalet Rose

Morez

Bois-d'Amont

Gros Crétet (1299m)

Roche Blanche △

Les Rousses

▲ Mont Pelé (1532m)

SWITZERLAND

Bief de la Chaille

La Cure

St-Cergue

to Lausanne

Couvaloup de St-Cergue

La Dôle (1677m)

N90

Trélex

Crêt Pela (1495m)

to Geneva

Nyon Lake Geneva

SECTION 11
Les Hôpitaux-Neufs to Nyon

Start	Les Hôpitaux-Neufs
Distance	86.5km (53.5 miles)
Maps	IGN TOP100 sheet 143; TOP75 sheet 012

Les Hôpitaux-Neufs to Le Morond, 4km (2.5 miles), 1hr 30min

Campsite, chambres d'hôtes, restaurants, café/bar and shops in Les Hôpitaux-Neufs; hotels, restaurants, cafés and shops in Métabief (1km off-route); bar/restaurant in Le Petit Morond; refuge in Le Gros Morond.

Turn right along the road towards Métabief, then left along the road opposite La Poste, Rue de la Sablière. Continue up Rue des Combettes, and at the top go right, along a footpath marked 'sentier piéton'. On reaching a track, turn right and continue along the side of the hill to a T-junction at Rebillet. Turn left, and at the Pouillet junction, take the track to the right, but immediately take a footpath to the right. Cross a pasture and enter the woods again, then at the next clearing turn right on a track along the edge of the trees to meet a road. Turn left, then follow signs up Sentier du Morond to the right. Be aware that mountain bike tracks criss-cross the route up to the summit.

Soon after passing under a bridge, at Le Petit Balcon, take a footpath left, climbing steeply through woods to reach a road. Cross over and continue up the route opposite to a ski run, where Sentier du Morond is signed to the right.

At the top, take a stony footpath to the left to an information board looking out over the valley. The GR5 crosses the pasture to the right and goes through a tunnel to the Chalet du Petit Morond. Join a gravel track uphill, then continue along a path to re-enter woods. The footpath becomes quite steep but soon reaches a road. Follow the road uphill as it swings round to the summit of **Le Morond** (1419m).

> From the summit of **Le Morond** there is a distant panorama of the Alps, and it is possible to see Mont Blanc. In the other direction, the peaks of Mont Suchet and Aiguilles de Baulmes in the Swiss Jura catch the eye. Nearer to hand the course of the GR5 winds along the crest towards Le Mont d'Or, following the top of the east-facing cliffs.

Le Morond to La Boissaude, 5km (3 miles), 1hr 45min
Auberge (refreshments) in La Boissaude.

Leave the summit towards Le Mont d'Or, following a fence, then turning right. Take this path downhill to a small lake, where the route goes to the right, to pass through an information shelter. Le Gros Morond refuge is to the right, but the route continues up the opposite slope to a gravel track. Turn right. There are warnings about the dangerous drop but the path steers well clear of the edge, and for the next 0.5km gives fine views over the cliffs.

The path emerges onto a car park, where a short detour leads up to the summit of **Le Mont d'Or** (1460m).

> Three hundred Alpine peaks are said to be visible from the summit of **Le Mont d'Or**. The Swiss border is only a short distance away, and it is possible to follow footpaths down into Switzerland and the facilities of Vallorbe. There is a good chance of seeing chamois on this section of the crest if there is not too much disturbance, and Alpine flowers grow in profusion.

Stay on the road from the car park for about 0.5km then leave to the left. ▶ Cross a track and a road and pass a farmstead at La Blonay. At the next road the chalet-restaurant **La Boissaude** is to the right.

Watch out: there are waymarks (both red/white for the GR and blue/yellow), but neither these marks, nor the path, are very obvious.

La Boissaude to Mouthe, 11.5km (7 miles), 3hr 30min
*Chambres d'hôtes, gîte, campsite, restaurants,
cafés and shops in Mouthe.*

Cross the road and continue through the pasture to an
access gap in a wall. From here the route goes downhill,
then swings left into the woods. Turn right on reaching a
road, and pass Les Granges Raguin. Very soon look out
for a track to the left and follow this just inside the woods,
then fork right to cross a cattle grid into pasture. This
winds past a barn at Le Corneau and leads into forest.

When the track becomes less obvious, continue
across a pasture and back into trees. At a turnstile turn
right and follow this track as it twists and turns, with clear
waymarking. After going through a narrow access gap the
path goes downhill through beech woods. On emerging
from the trees, cross a lane by the farm of La Vannode,
and follow the field edge to a stile. Cross the next field,
and head for a large wooden stile leading over a wall into
woodland.

At the next junction the GR5 goes right, and then
leaves the woods just before **Grange Bousson**. Go past
the farmstead, and cross into the field opposite, where
waymarks lead across fields towards a row of beech
trees. Continue down a woodland track to reach a lane
at Sapeau Léger. Turn right and almost immediately, at
a sharp right-hand bend, take the path left. Turn left at
a T-junction to follow a clearly marked track twisting
through the trees. At a road turn downhill to a hairpin
where a waymarked vehicle track leaves straight ahead to
meet another road.

Continue downhill to a junction, which overlooks
the town of Mouthe spread out along the valley floor
ahead. Turn left, then immediately right, following a path
as it twists through the trees and under ski-lifts to reach a
well-made footpath. The GR5 turns right, while the steps
to the left go up to a viewpoint over the source of the
Doubs.

The route emerges at the **Source du Doubs**, and continues to a junction in front of a campsite. Turn left then

follow the footpath along the riverbank into **Mouthe**. On entering the town, go left, past the church, to the main street.

> The position of **Mouthe**, at close to 1000m of altitude and sitting at a low point relative to surrounding land, has earned it a unique reputation as 'La Petite Sibérie'. In winter a layer of cold air can accumulate here, resulting in some very low temperatures indeed. It holds the record as the coldest commune in all France, with a low of −36.7°C on 13 January 1968.

Mouthe

Mouthe to Chaux-Neuve, 7.5km (4.5 miles), 2hr 15min
Hotel and shop in Chaux-Neuve.

Turn left along the main street and left down the D389 at the edge of town. After 0.5km the GR5 leaves to the right following a broad track. Within about 10min the main track heads off towards the left and the route follows a minor track that carries on ahead to cross a small wooden bridge then enter woods.

Pass a path to Moulin Cagnard, and about 5min later a broader track joins from the left. Follow this to the right to reach a lane and continue straight on. Turn right at a T-junction, and follow the road around a left-hand bend. As the road turns to the right, leave obliquely to the left along a vehicle track. The route leads along the side of a valley and eventually drops to cross a small stream. Not long after, where the track takes a sharp right turn, leave by a footpath on the bend.

The route crosses a lane leading to Hameau Vuillet. Stay with the track, which soon leads up the bank to the right, then cross a stile into a field. Turn left and follow the fence towards **Chaux-Neuve**.

Pass the Auberge du Grand Git, then join a minor road and follow this around to the right to the D437. Turn left, then left again down Grande Rue.

**Chaux-Neuve to Chapelle-des-Bois,
13.5km (8.5 miles), 4hr 15min**
Hotel/restaurants, gîte and shop in Chapelle-des-Bois.

Follow Grande Rue out of the village, cross a bridge and turn right down Le Lernier. After this road ends, continue across pasture to join a lane, then turn left to a signpost. Take the track to the right, but very soon go down a foot-path on the right, by an old barn. Turn left by the ruins of a farm. The path follows the forest edge, then goes through woods to pass an isolated stone building before reaching a road, where the GR5 goes left.

The road climbs steadily for about 2.5km, passing signs to Les Enguenelles, Grande Combe and Pré d'Haut.

Cross a large clearing soon after, and leave by the left-hand track. Fork right, then at a multi-trunked beech tree, follow the track to the left. Join another track and continue straight on. The route takes a downhill fork, towards Chapelle-des-Bois. Only a few minutes later fork left to a T-junction and turn left downhill.

The track curves right, and at the signpost at Grand Tartet, go right to reach a road. Follow the track opposite as it curves left to a fine, open viewpoint. Drop to the left of this, and continue down through scattered trees then turn to re-enter woods. Turn left at the next junction and follow waymarks along this track, passing a farm to reach a T-junction and turn left into **Chapelle-des-Bois**.

> Just 1.5km outside Chapelle-des-Bois is **La Distillerie Michel**, founded in 1888 and still a thriving producer of liqueurs from gentian roots. The plants in question are not the tiny, blue-flowered rockery alpines, but tall-growing yellow gentians abundant in many of the pastures. As they can reach up to 2m high, they need a substantial root system for support, and it is this root that is harvested. When taken as an aperitif or liqueur, the extract is said to be an effective tonic and stimulant.

Chapelle-des-Bois to Roche Bernard, 4.5km (3 miles), 2hr
Gîte and refreshments in Chalet Gaillard (1.5km off-route).

Turn right, past the church and village shop, then left along Chemin des Sources, which winds between pastures, passing a metal cross marking a plague burial. When the road takes a sharp right-hand bend, leave to the left.

This stony track crosses pasture to enter woods. When it turns sharply right, take a path straight ahead, then continue left along a track. In the next field, a sign to Roche Champion points uphill, alongside a rough wall. The path hairpins steeply up through the trees. When the ground flattens at the top, ignore the distinct path ahead as the correct route turns sharply right.

*Approaching
Roche Champion*

Soon after a turn off
to a nearby viewpoint
at Git de l'Échelle,
there is a memorial
to wartime refugees
who escaped across
this border into
Switzerland.

The path contours for some distance, heading along the ridge. This leads on through trees to reach the lookout area of **Belvédère de la Roche Champion**. There is an enormous cross here and a superb view.

Take the path towards Roche Bernard, which leaves along the clifftop, soon forking right. This little rocky footpath meanders through woods, following waymarks, and passing close to some border stones. ◄

On reaching a junction, where a left turn heads for **Chalet Gaillard**, turn right, and at the Croisée des Roches junction, **Roche Bernard** is indicated left, up a rocky path.

Roche Bernard to Chalet Rose,
7.5km (4.5 miles), 2hr 30min
Rough shelter in Le Plan Perrat.

The path continues along the ridge, forking left at the Les Essarts signpost. Within 10min the route is diverted right, and a few minutes later joins a track, and follows it down to the right, to a clearing at Le Plan Perrat. Turn right towards Chemin Neuf.

Pass an unlocked shelter, then at the next junction, Le Chemin Neuf, turn left towards Le Chalet Rose. This leads through forest for about 20min, reaching a road at Le Plan des Buchaillers. Turn right and continue for a little over 1km, and at Carrefour du Capucin turn left to Carrefour du Plan Pichon.

Turn right, and follow this track to Carrefour de la Biche. Turn right, downhill, and continue along the road for 5min to **Chalet Rose**, a locked shelter.

Chalet Rose to Les Rousses, 7km (4 miles), 2hr
Hotels, gîte, restaurants, café/bars and shops in Les Rousses.

Take a rough vehicle track on the left, passing a small quarry, and continue for about half an hour, then turn left at Combe Sèche. Ignore side paths until the junction at **Gros Crêtet** (1299m) about 1km away. The GR5 leaves to the right along a vehicle track, and a few minutes later branches left.

At the next junction, a diversion to the viewpoint of **Roche Blanche** 20min away, is well worthwhile (yellow waymarks). To keep with the GR5, turn left downhill.

At a junction, cross a major track, and continue straight on to meet another. Turn left, and where this track ends at La Loge à Ponard, a path continues downhill, which later joins a rough track, and arrives at the road at Le Grépillon. Turn left along this road into Les Rousse-en-Bas.

The main part of **Les Rousses** still lies ahead – the church can be seen on the crest of the hill. To reach it go right, down Rue du Préchavin. Follow the road down, then turn left up a steep little path that climbs to rejoin the road. Turn left and left again by a fromagerie, to go along Rue Pasteur, passing a variety of cafés and shops to reach the tourist office.

Les Rousses to La Cure, 6km (4 miles), 2hr
Gîte in La Grenotte; hotel, gîte and restaurants in La Cure.

Cross the road at the tourist office and turn right, then soon left up to the Fort des Rousses. Walk along the rampart, then drop down to the right, signposted to Bief de la Chaille, to reach a lane. Turn right, but immediately sharply left onto a footpath to reach Les Entrepreneurs. Take a footpath to the right, through the outer ramparts, down to Le Sagy-Haut.

Go down the lane opposite, pass an isolated house then, at the Le Bonzon signpost, carry on towards Bief de la Chaille. After about 10min, turn right at the Sous le Saut junction, and follow signs to the **Bief de la Chaille waterfall** in a shaded little gorge.

The view opens out, with the radar dome on La Dôle (1677m) in Switzerland in the distance.

Climb up, following waymarks along the road. ◀ Turn right, along a minor road and follow this downhill. It crosses a stream and turns right, but the route carries on ahead along a vehicle track leading uphill, passing the gîte d'étape La Grenotte, and reaching the D29.

The GR5 turns left along the road, but note that other red and white waymarks lead to the right. At Les Piles, leave along a side road to the right, and follow this to rejoin the main road a few minutes later. Continue straight on and cross a roundabout to go into **La Cure**.

View back over the French Jura

La Cure is truly a frontier village, part being in France and part in Switzerland. The division does

not only apply to the village as a whole – some individual buildings have the border running through them. This is taken to extremes in the Franco-Swiss Hotel Arbez, where one of the rooms has a double bed with the two sides lying in different countries.

La Cure to St-Cergue, 8.5km (5.5 miles), 2hr 40min
Hotel/gîte in La Givrine; hotels, campsite, restaurants, cafés and shops in St-Cergue.

To follow the GR5 into Switzerland, turn right, passing the Swiss customs post, then continue up the road. The waymarking for the GR changes from here, with all walking routes waymarked with a yellow diamond. Signposts either use place names or the words *tourisme pédestre*, but there are no references to the GR5.

Follow the main road for about 0.4km, and look out for yellow diamond signs to the left. Turn up Route de la Bouriaz, and then left along a footpath beside the railway. The path soon comes down to cross a road. Take the wide vehicle track opposite towards Nyon. Follow this forest track for about 1km, ignoring a turn off to the right, and just as it becomes a road, turn right. This leads through a gateway towards a group of buildings, and reaches a signpost at La Pile-Dessus. Turn left and set off across open pasture in the direction indicated; there is hardly any footpath.

This meets a vehicle track at a signpost; follow this left. The track begins to fade, but carry on. Another signpost comes into view near the forest edge, on a wide vehicle track. Turn left towards La Trélasse. The track leads to a stone wall near a main road. Turn right to follow the path running parallel to the wall, passing a sign for La Givrine.

Cross a lane and carry on downhill, following a clearing with tall trees on either side. The route then follows a faint vehicle track left, curving up towards the buildings of **Couvaloup de St-Cergue**. Currently there is no sign, so take care to go up to the left of these buildings, to reach the road at a junction. Cross over and take the St-Cergue track as indicated. Follow this down a narrow clearing between conifers. Fork right at a signposted junction in the forest, to emerge onto a road.

Follow this downhill, between chalets, and turn right at a T-junction. A little further on, leave to the left, following a lane into the woods. This leads onto a footpath that crosses a large field, then runs alongside a powerline before dropping left to a road.

Turn right, passing the St-Cergue campsite. When the road meets the main road, take Chemin de la Vieille Route to the right. On the edge of **St-Cergue** branch off along Chemin Jacques Rousseau to the main street.

DÉSALPE

St-Cergue is one of the Jura villages that maintains the annual Désalpe celebrations that mark the return of cattle from the high pastures. The leading cows are decorated with colourful headdresses and driven down through the village street, and the farmers, in traditional attire, seem to enjoy the occasion. The event usually falls on a Saturday in late September or early October, when the street is lined with a variety of stalls and there is a holiday atmosphere.

St-Cergue to Trélex, 6.5km (4 miles), 2hr
Restaurant and shop in Trélex.

Turn right and leave the village alongside the main road. Beyond a hotel/restaurant the GR5 leaves by the second track on the left, going steeply downhill. This broad track, an old Roman road, drops through woods and within 3km crosses the main road six times, cutting across the various hairpin bends.

After the last road crossing, the track forks. Follow the signs to the left to emerge onto a minor road. Turn left to follow this into **Trélex** and go down a lane on the left to reach the main street.

Trélex to Nyon, 5km (3 miles), 1hr 30min
Hotels and range of facilities and shops in Nyon.

Cross the main street and go down Coin Greinge. Turn left down Route de la Gare, and left again to cross the railway line and follow the little road opposite, taking the track between fields ahead. At two isolated trees, fork left, and at a crossroads take the track opposite, which leads beneath a busy highway. Join a road at a corner, carry straight on and follow this as it turns right. Turn left very soon after, following the yellow waymarks along a long, straight road, which becomes Chemin de Changins.

The old Roman road above Nyon

Turn right along Chemin du Groseiller, then left along Route de St-Cergue towards the centre of **Nyon**. At the end of this road, take the pedestrian way under the railway to Place de la Gare, then cross to Rue de la Gare almost opposite. Carry straight on through the pedestrianised area, then turn left along Place Bel-Air and go down Ruelle des Moulins, entering an older part of town and passing the castle.

Follow this alley as it turns left, then turn left at Rue de Rive, and finally right, down to the shore of **Lake Geneva** and the embarkation point for the lake ferries. If you plan to travel on from Geneva or its airport, return to Nyon station for a direct train.

The shore of Lake Geneva

The GR5 carries on from St-Gingolph on the far side of the lake, and taking a ferry is a relaxing way to cross, but it is not direct and could involve an extra overnight stop. Taking a train to Lausanne, then the ferry, is quicker. Ahead lie a further 660km through the French Alps to reach the end of the GR5 in Nice.

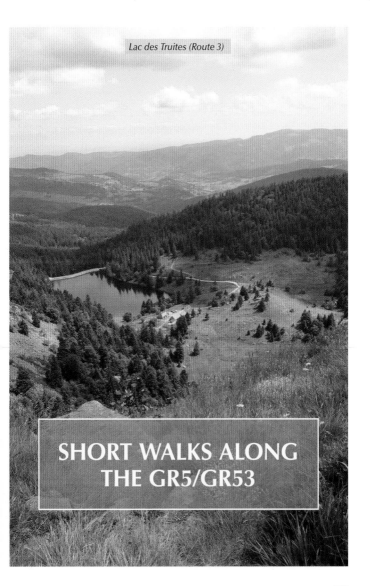

Lac des Truites (Route 3)

SHORT WALKS ALONG
THE GR5/GR53

Some of the finest stretches of the GR5 and GR53 can be enjoyed as day walks, and the circuits suggested below incorporate some particularly recommended sections. While the GR5/GR53 is well waymarked and described elsewhere in this guide, some of the return parts of these circuits may not be so easy to follow without a map.

SHORT WALK 1
Castles of the Northern Vosges

Start/finish	Fleckenstein Campsite
Distance	12km (7.5 miles)
Total ascent	440m
Time	3hr
Maps	TOP100, No 112; TOP75, No 027 (or Club Vosgien 1:50,000, sheet 2/8)

From the campsite at Étang du Fleckenstein take the small forestry road opposite (signposted 'Gimbelhof') to the GR53 at the Col du Litschhof. Follow the GR53 for 5.5km (Section 1), passing castles at Loewenstein and **Fleckenstein** to reach **Froensbourg**.

Sandstone crags at Froensbourg Castle

Return by going back along the GR53 to the end of the Étang du Fleckenstein, then turn right, along the D925 back to the starting point.

SHORT WALK 2
Haut-Barr Castle

Start/finish	Saverne
Distance	21.5km (13.5 miles)
Total ascent	710m
Time	5hr 30min
Maps	TOP100, No 112; TOP75, No 027 (or Club Vosgien 1:50,000, sheet 1/8)

The 9km stretch of the GR53 south from Saverne (Section 3) passes several castle ruins, the most striking being **Haut-Barr**. Continue to the junction at Haberacker. From here the GR531 (blue rectangles) can be used for the return route, passing **Ochsenstein** and Greifenstein Castles on the way back to Saverne.

SHORT WALK 3
Gazon du Faing

Start/finish	Col du Calvaire (with parking)
Distance	15.5km (9.5 miles)
Total ascent	430m
Time	4hr 30min
Maps	TOP100, No 122; TOP, No 028 (or Club Vosgien 1:50,000, sheet 6/8, recommended)

From **Col du Calvaire** follow the GR5 south (Section 5) along the crest as far as Collet du Lac Vert, then take the red disc route down to Lac Vert to follow yellow disc waymarks back to Lac des Truites.

Cross the dam and follow the red discs towards Lac Noir. After about 25min, when Lac Noir is in sight below, watch out for the red/white/red route crossing the track. Turn right to **Lac Noir**, and join the GR532 (yellow rectangles), which leaves by the road then climbs the bank to the left. Continue along the GR532 to **Lac Blanc**, (possible detour to visit the belvédère), then on to rejoin the GR5 close to Col du Calvaire.

SHORT WALK 4
Le Hohneck

Start/finish	Mittlach, west of Munster, or Le Hohneck (summit parking)
Distance	19km (12 miles)
Total ascent	930m
Time	5hr 30min
Maps	TOP100, No 122; TOP75, No 028 (or Club Vosgien 1:50,000, sheet 6/8)

Col du Herrenberg

From Mittlach take the GR5 south-west (Section 6) to the **Col du Herrenberg**. Turn right, along the ridge, using the alternative route (red/white/red), passing **Le Rainkopf** and **Le Kastelberg**. At Le Hohneck pick up the GR5 again (Section 5) to drop back down to Mittlach, passing Lac Schiessrothried and Lac Fischboedle.

SHORT WALK 5
Le Grand Ballon

Start/finish	Col du Haag, on the Route des Crêtes
Distance	14.5km (9 miles)
Total ascent	460m
Time	4hr
Maps	TOP100, No 122; TOP75, No 028 (or Club Vosgien 1:50,000, sheet 6/8, recommended)

From **Col du Haag** the GR5 crosses the summit of Le Grand Ballon (Section 6) then drops down past the Ferme-Auberge du Ballon. Just over 0.5km from here, leave the GR5 and take the blue cross route to the left to Judenhut. Follow this path past Judenhut towards Gustiberg.

About 15min beyond Lieserwasen the blue cross path divides. Take the left branch onwards to Gustiberg, and continue to **Lac du Ballon**. Go across the dam and take the red/white/red path uphill and through the parking area, and towards Col du Haag. This zigzags upwards. Turn left on reaching the GR532 (yellow rectangles) to return to Col du Haag.

SHORT WALK 6
Saut du Doubs

Start/finish	The car park at the Châtelot Barrage, reached by road through Le Barboux and Le Pissoux
Distance	12km (7.5 miles)
Total ascent	400m
Time	3hr
Maps	IGN TOP100, No 137

From the car park go down the steps and follow the GR5 south (Section 9) to **Saut du Doubs**. Carry on from the waterfall towards the embarkation point for boat trips, and take the road uphill. Leave the GR5 at the Les Vions sign, go straight ahead alongside a car park, then keep straight on to a T-junction. Follow the minor road to the right to **Le Pissoux**. From the village carry straight on, pick up the GR5 route, and go down to the car park by the dam.

SHORT WALK 7
Le Morond and Le Mont d'Or

Start/finish	Métabief (parking by ski-lifts)
Distance	9km (5.5 miles)
Total ascent	550m
Time	3hr 30min
Maps	IGN TOP100, No 137; TOP75, No 012

This short walk returns by the outward route. Starting from the parking by the ski centre in Métabief, walk uphill, and take the road to the left, signed Sentier du Morond. Follow this quiet road for about 0.7km and turn right, up the GR5 (Section 11). Follow this for about 4km

Cliffs at Le Mont d'Or

over **Le Morond** to reach the cliffs by **Le Mont d'Or**. A short diversion reaches the summit itself. To return to Métabief, retrace your steps back to the car park.

SHORT WALK 8
Roche Bernard

Start/finish	Chapelle-des-Bois, between Mouthe and Les Rousses
Distance	9.5km (6 miles)
Total ascent	210m
Time	3hr
Maps	IGN TOP100, No143; TOP75, No 012

The 4.5km of the GR5 south from **Chapelle-des-Bois** (Section 11) includes a steep climb to the ridge of Mont Risoux, passing the outlook point of **Roche Champion** to reach **Roche Bernard**. A return route is possible by retracing the path for a short distance to the signpost at Croisée des Roches and turning left towards Sur les Lacs. This descends steeply to join a quiet road where you turn right and return to Chapelle-des-Bois.

APPENDIX A

Long distance routes in the Vosges and Jura

The Vosges

In addition to the GR5/GR53 there are several other long distance routes in the Vosges. The GR531 and GR532 both run north–south, and combining sections of these two routes with parts of the main GR5/GR53 allows many circular trips to be considered. The outlines below are not detailed, but offer ideas that might help in planning a trip. Precise routes are on the TOP100 maps for the Vosges.

The GR531

The GR531 (waymarked by blue rectangles) extends from Soultz-sous-Forêts to the Swiss border at Leymen. The 281km (174.5 miles) of this route through the Vosges as far as Masevaux showcases many aspects of the Vosgien landscape. Compared with the more important GR5/GR53, some well-known landmarks are bypassed (such as Le Grand Ballon), but there are many other highlights. The route incorporates the excellent viewpoints on Le Grand Ventron and Le Petit Drumont, and passes through the town of Munster in the valley of the Fecht.

The GR532

The GR532 (waymarked by yellow rectangles) is another alternative 367km (230-mile) north–south route in the Vosges from Wissembourg to Belfort that leads the walker past a different selection of points of interest as it crosses and recrosses the GR5/GR53 and GR531. Particular highlights include many attractive towns and villages, such as Turckheim and St-Amarin, and open views gained from such summits as Grand Brézouard (1228m) and Le Petit Ballon (1267m). The route now extends beyond Belfort to Mulhouse.

The Jura

In addition to the GR5, sections of the GTJ, GR9, GR59 and several other routes all cross the Jura. There are also several GR de Pays circuits which in total cover a large part of the region. Of the many possibilities for long distance routes, two have been chosen for special mention here. The outlines below are not detailed, but offer ideas that might help in planning a trip. Precise routes are on the TOP100 maps for the Jura.

The GTJ (Grande Traversée du Jura)

The GTJ starts near Montbéliard and extends down to Culoz, in the extreme south of the French Jura. North of La Cure, the route often coincides with the GR5, but to the south the GTJ continues for a further 135km (84 miles), crossing some higher elevations and reaching the Crêt de la Neige at 1720m, the highest point in the Jura. It drops steeply to Bellegarde-sur-Valserine before rising again to cross the Plateau de Retord, then descending sharply to Culoz.

The GR59

The GR59 stretches from the Ballon d'Alsace in the Vosges to connect with the GR9 at Yenne, south of Geneva. As a north–south route from Vosges to Jura, it might be thought of as a rival to the GR5, but the two routes are very different. The GR59 maintains a more westerly course, exploring a scenic area of plateau edge and broad, flat, steep-sided valleys that form a picturesque and interesting landscape.

While the GR59 in its entirety would prove a rewarding journey, the 94km (58-mile) section from Salins-les-Bains, through Arbois, to Lons-le-Saunier includes some of the best limestone scenery and is a good introduction to the area.

APPENDIX B
Route summary tables

Long distance routes

GR53

	Start	Finish	Distance	Ascent/descent	Time	Page
Section 1	Wissembourg	Niederbronn-les-Bains	45km (28 miles)	1390m/1370m	14hr 35min	28
Section 2	Niederbronn-les-Bains	Saverne	54km (33.5 miles)	1250m/1240m	17hr	39
Section 3	Saverne	Schirmeck	70.5km (44 miles)	2260m/2130m	23hr	53
		Total	**169.5km (105.5 miles)**	**4900m/4740m**	**54hr 35min**	

GR5

	Start	Finish	Distance	Ascent/descent	Time	Page
Section 4	Schirmeck	Ribeauvillé	86.5km (54 miles)	2730m/2810m	28hr	69
Section 5	Ribeauvillé	Mittlach	54km (33.5 miles)	2060m/1770m	18hr	84
Section 6	Mittlach	Thann	40.5km (25 miles)	1170m/1360m	13hr 10min	96
Section 7	Thann	Brévilliers	68.5km (42.5 miles)	1740m/1715m	21hr 50min	107
Section 8	Brévilliers	St-Hippolyte	47km (29 miles)	860m/780m	13hr 50min	122
Section 9	St-Hippolyte	Viller-le-Lac	71km (44 miles)	1470m/1260m	21hr 45min	133

Long distance routes					
	Start	Finish	Distance	Ascent/descent	Time	Page
Section 10	Viller-le-Lac	Les Hôpitaux-Neufs	64km (39.5 miles)	1460m/1190m	19hr 45min	146
Section 11	Les Hôpitaux-Neufs	Nyon	86.5km (53.5 miles)	1170m/1740m	27hr 55min	159
		Total	**518km (322 miles)**	**12,660m/12,625m**	**164hr 15min**	
		Total for GR53 and GR5	**687.5km (427 miles)**	**17,560m/17,365m**	**218hr 50min**	

Short Walks along the GR5/GR53				
	Start/finish	Distance	Total ascent	Time	Page
Short walk 1	Fleckenstein campsite	12km (7.5 miles)	440m	3hr	176
Short walk 2	Saverne	21.5km (13.5 miles)	710m	5hr 30min	177
Short walk 3	Col du Calvaire	15.5km (9.5 miles)	430m	4hr 30min	177
Short walk 4	Mittlach or Le Hohneck	19km (12 miles)	930m	5hr 30min	178
Short walk 5	Col du Haag	14.5km (9 miles)	460m	4hr	179
Short walk 6	Châtelot Barrage	12km (7.5 miles)	400m	3hr	180
Short walk 7	Métabief	9km (5.5 miles)	550m	3hr 30min	180
Short walk 8	Chapelle-des-Bois	9.5km (6 miles)	210m	3hr	181

APPENDIX C
Facilities table

Where facilities lie off-route, the middle columns give the distance to the turn-off point from the main route.

	Km	Cumulative km	Facilities
Section 1 GR53 Wissembourg to Niederbronn-les-Bains			
Wissembourg	0	0	Hotels, restaurants, cafés, shops
Scherhol summit	5	5	Shelter
Col du Pigeonnier	0.5	5.5	Refuge
Climbach	3	8.5	Hotel/restaurants, baker
Petit-Wingen	2.5	11	Restaurant
Fleckenstein Castle	6.5	17.5	Café
Fleckenstein Campsite (1km off-route)	1	18.5	Campsite
Obersteinbach	9.5	28	Hotels, gîte, restaurants
Windstein	5.5	33.5	Hotel/restaurant, chambres d'hôtes
Niederbronn	11.5	45	Hotels, campsite, restaurants, cafés, shops
Section 2 GR53 Niederbronn-les-Bains to Saverne			
Niederbronn	0	0	Hotels, campsite, restaurants, cafés, shops
Muhlthal	11	11	Restaurant (high class)
Lichtenberg	7.5	18.5	Hotels/restaurants, gîte
Wimmenau	6	24.5	Hotel/restaurant, shops
La Petite-Pierre	10.5	35	Hotels, gîte, restaurants, cafés, baker
Imsthal	2.5	37.5	Campsite, hotel/restaurant
Graufthal	4.5	42	Hotel, restaurants
Oberhof	3.5	45.5	Bar/restaurant
Saverne	8.5	54	Hotels, youth hostel, campsite, restaurants, cafés, shops
Section 3 GR53 Saverne to Schirmeck			
Saverne	0	0	Hotels, youth hostel, campsite, restaurants, cafés, shops
Haut-Barr	3	3	Café/restaurant

	Km	Cumulative km	Facilities
La Hoube (0.5km off-route)	11	14	Hotel/restaurant
Dabo	2.5	16.5	Gîte, campsite, turn off for Dabo village
Dabo village (1.5km off-route)			Restaurant, cafés, shop
Col de la Schleif	2.5	19	Shelter
Engenthal (1km off-route)	1.5	20.5	Gîte
Wangenbourg (1km off-route)	3.5	24	Hotels, campsite, restaurants, baker/café
Schneeberg (0.5km off-route)	3.5	27.5	Shelter
Nideck (D218)	5.5	33	Café/gîte
Luttenbach (Note: avoid confusion with Luttenbach near Munster)	2	35	Gîte, campsite
Oberhaslach (1km off-route)	2	37	Hotel/restaurants, shops
Urmatt	3.5	40.5	Hotels, restaurants, shops
Col du Donon	22.5	63	Hotels, restaurants
Wackenbach	6	69	Chambres d'hôtes
Schirmeck	1.5	70.5	Restaurants, cafés, shops, turn off for La Claquette
La Claquette (3km off-route)			Hotel, hostel
Section 4 GR5 Schirmeck to Ribeauvillé			
Schirmeck	0	0	Restaurants, cafés, shops, turn off for La Claquette
La Claquette (3km off-route)			Hotel, hostel
Struthof	5	5	Restaurant (0.5km before Struthof)
La Serva (1.5km off-route)	10.5	15.5	Hotel/restaurant
Chaume des Veaux (1km off-route)		15.5	Refuge
Le Hohwald	6.5	22	Hotels/restaurants, gîte, campsite, cafés, shop

	Km	Cumulative km	Facilities
Mont Ste-Odile	9.5	31.5	Hotel (at convent), café/restaurant
Barr	8	39.5	Hotels, campsite, restaurants, cafés, shops
Mittelbergheim (0.5km off-route)	1.5	41	Hotel, restaurants
Andlau	2	43	Hotels, restaurants, cafés, shops
Gruckert	4	47	Refuge
Reichsfeld (1km off-route)		47	Chambres d'hôtes
Châtenois	20.5	67.5	Hotels, gîte, restaurants, cafés, shops
La Wick	5	72.5	Café
Haut-Koenigsbourg	4	76.5	Café/restaurant, snack stall
Thannenkirch	4	80.5	Hotels, café/restaurants, shop
Ribeauvillé	6	86.5	Hotels, campsites, restaurants, cafés, shops

Section 5 GR5 Ribeauvillé to Mittlach

	Km	Cumulative km	Facilities
Ribeauvillé	0	0	Hotels, campsites, restaurants, cafés, shops
Aubure	10.5	10.5	Restaurant
Pierre des Trois-Bans	5	15.5	Shelter
Col des Bagenelles	8	23.5	Refuge, ferme-auberge
Le Bonhomme	2.5	26	Hotels, campsite, gîte, restaurants, café/bar, shops
Étang du Devin	2.5	28.5	Hotel/gîte
Col du Calvaire	5.5	34	Hotel, refuge, café/restaurant
Gazon du Faing (0.5km off-route)	4	38	Ferme-auberge
Schanzwasen (1.5km off-route)	2	40	Auberge/hotel
Col de la Schlucht	4	44	Hotel, restaurants
Trois-Fours	1.5	45.5	Refuge/gîte, ferme-auberge
Sotré (1km off-route)	1.5	47	Refuge
Le Hohneck	0.5	47.5	Restaurant, auberge/hotels
Schiessroth	1.5	49	Ferme-auberge
Metzeral (3km off-route)	4	53	Hotels, shops

	Km	Cumulative km	Facilities
Mittlach	1	54	Chambres d'hôtes, turn off for Langenwasen
Langenwasen (2.5km off-route)			Campsite
Section 6 GR5 Mittlach to Thann			
Mittlach	0	0	Chambres d'hôtes, turn off for Langenwasen
Langenwasen (2.5km off-route)			Campsite
Col du Herrenberg	6	6	Ferme-auberge
Col d'Hannenbrunnen	4	10	Ferme-auberge
Le Markstein	4.5	14.5	Hotels, gîte, refuges, café/restaurants
Col du Haag	7	21.5	Ferme-auberge
Le Grand Ballon	1.5	23	Hotel, restaurants/cafés
Ferme du Ballon	2	25	Ferme-auberge
Molkenrain	8	33	Refuge, ferme-auberge/refuge
Thann	7.5	40.5	Hotels, gîte, restaurants, cafés, shops
Section 7 GR5 Thann to Brévilliers			
Thann	0	0	Hotels, gîte, restaurants, cafés, shops
Col du Hundsruck	6.5	6.5	Hotel/restaurant
Thannerhubel (off-route)	1	7.5	Ferme-auberge/refuge
Belacker	5	12.5	Ferme-auberge/gîte
Rouge Gazon (1km off-route)	6	18.5	Auberge/hotel/gîte
Gazon Vert (off-route)		18.5	Auberge/gîte
Petite Chaume (0.3km off-route)	4	22.5	Shelter
Ballon d'Alsace (road)	5	27.5	Hotel, ferme-auberge/chambres d'hôtes, restaurant
Auberge des Moraines (just off-route)	7	34.5	Chambres d'hôtes
Lepuix	3	37.5	Shop
Giromagny	2	39.5	Hotel, gîte, restaurants, cafés, shops
Lachapelle-sous-Chaux	7	46.5	Chambres d'hôtes
Évette	4	50.5	Restaurant, café/bar

	Km	Cumulative km	Facilities
Châlonvillars	8.5	59	Restaurant
Héricourt (3km off-route)	9.5	68.5	Hotel, restaurants, cafés, shops
Section 8 GR5 Brévilliers to St-Hippolyte			
Héricourt (3km off-route)	0	0	Hotel, restaurants, cafés, shops
Châtenois-les-Forges	6.5	6.5	Restaurant, café, shops
Étupes (3km off-route)	7	13.5	Hotel
Fesches-le-Châtel (2km off-route)	1.5	15	Restaurants, cafés, shops
Dasle	6.5	21.5	Restaurant, shop
Vandoncourt	1.5	23	Restaurant, shop
Abbévillers	4.5	27.5	Baker
Hérimoncourt (2km off-route)		27.5	Bus route giving access to facilities in Audincourt and Montbéliard
La Papeterie	3.5	31	Restaurant
Chamesol	12	43	Restaurant
St-Hippolyte (just off-route)	4	47	Hotels, campsite, restaurants, cafés, shops
Section 9 St-Hippolyte to Villers-le-Lac			
St-Hippolyte (just off-route)	0	0	Hotels, campsite, restaurants, cafés, shops
Courtefontaine	9.5	9.5	Bar/restaurant
Fessevillers	7.5	17	Gîte
Goumois	7	24	Hotel, campsite, café/restaurants, shop
Bief d'Etoz	5.5	29.5	Restaurant (La Goule, Switzerland)
La Charbonnière	5	34.5	Shelter
Bois de la Biche (1.5km off-route)	2.5	37	Hotel
Le Refrain, parking	0.5	37.5	Shelter (old chapel)
Biaufond (0.5km off-route)	6	43.5	Gîte
La Rasse	1	44.5	Hotel/restaurant
Abri du Torret	7.5	52	Shelter
Saut du Doubs	12	64	Café, restaurant, snack stalls

	Km	Cumulative km	Facilities
Le Cerneux Billard (3km off-route)	1	65	Gîte
Villers-le-Lac	6	71	Hotels, gîte, restaurants, cafés, shops
Section 10 GR5 Villers-le-Lac to Les Hôpitaux-Neufs			
Villers-le-Lac	0	0	Hotels, gîte, restaurants, cafés, shops
Sur la Roche	5	5	Auberge/gîte
Vieux Châteleu	11.5	16.5	Auberge/gîte
Les Cerneux (1km off-route)	3	19.5	Auberge/gîte
Les Seignes	1.5	21	Chambres d'hôtes
Les Alliés	9.5	30.5	Gîte
La Perdrix (2km off-route)		30.5	Gîte
Le Larmont (1.5km off-route)	10.5	41	Campsite
Pontarlier (3km off-route)	2.5	43.5	Hotels, restaurants, cafés, shops
La Cluse-et-Mijoux	1.5	45	Restaurants, café/bar, baker
Les Fourgs	8	53	Chambres d'hôtes, shops, restaurant
Les Hôpitaux-Neufs	11	64	Campsite, chambres d'hôtes, restaurants, café/bar, shops
Métabief (1km off-route)		64	Hotels, restaurants, cafés, shops
Section 11 GR5 Les Hôpitaux-Neufs to Nyon			
Les Hôpitaux-Neufs	0	0	Campsite, restaurants, chambres d'hôtes, café/bar, shops
Métabief (1km off-route)	0	0	Hotels, restaurants, cafés, shops
Le Petit Morond	3	3	Bar/restaurant
Le Gros Morond	1	4	Refuge
La Boissaude	5	9	Auberge (refreshments)
Mouthe	11.5	20.5	Chambres d'hôtes, gîte, campsite, restaurants, cafés, shops
Chaux-Neuve	7.5	28	Hotel, shop
Chapelle-des-Bois	13.5	41.5	Hotel/restaurants, gîte, shop
Chalet Gaillard (1.5km off-route)	4	45.5	Gîte, refreshments
Le Plan Perrat	2	47.5	Rough shelter

	Km	Cumulative km	Facilities
Les Rousses	13	60.5	Hotels, gîte, restaurants, café/bars, shops
La Grenotte	4	64.5	Gîte
La Cure	2	66.5	Hotel, gîte, restaurants
La Givrine	4	70.5	Hotel/gîte
St-Cergue	4.5	75	Hotels, campsite, restaurants, cafés, shops
Trélex	6.5	81.5	Restaurant, shop
Nyon	5	86.5	Hotels, range of facilities and shops

APPENDIX D
Useful websites

Tourist information

General
North Alsace (Bas-Rhin)
www.tourisme67.com

Alsace
www.tourisme-alsace.com

Franche-Comté
www.franche-comte.org

French Regional Parks
www.parcs-naturels-regionaux.fr

Local tourist offices
Wissembourg
tel 03 88 94 10 11
www.ot-wissembourg.fr

Niederbronn-les-Bains
tel 03 88 80 89 70
www.niederbronn.com

La Petite-Pierre
tel 03 88 70 42 30
www.ot-paysdelapetitepierre.com

Saverne
tel 03 88 91 80 47
www.tourisme-saverne.fr

Dabo
tel 03 87 07 47 51
www.ot-dabo.fr

Wangenbourg
tel 03 88 87 33 50
www.suisse-alsace.fr

Oberhaslach
tel 03 88 50 90 15
www.commune-oberhaslach.fr

Schirmeck
tel 03 88 47 18 51
www.valleedelabruche.fr

Barr
tel 03 88 08 66 65
www.pays-de-barr.com

For Châtenois
tel 03 88 58 87 20
www.selestat-haut-koenigsbourg.com

Ribeauvillé
tel 03 89 73 23 23
www.ribeauville-riquewihr.com

Thann
tel 03 89 37 96 20
www.hautes-vosges-alsace.fr

St-Hippolyte
tel 03 81 96 58 00
www.tourisme-saint-hippolyte-doubs.fr

Villers-le-Lac
tel 03 81 68 00 98
www.pays-horloger.com

Pontarlier
tel 03 81 46 48 33
www.pontarlier.org

Métabief
tel 03 81 49 13 81
www.tourisme-metabief.com

Mouthe
tel 03 81 69 22 78
www.otmouthe.fr

Les Rousses
tel 03 84 60 02 55
www.lesrousses.com

St-Cergue
tel 0041 (0) 22 360 13 14
www.st-cergue-tourisme.ch

Nyon
tel 0041 (0) 22 365 66 00
www.nyon-tourisme.ch

Maps

Stanfords Mapsellers
www.stanfords.co.uk

The Map Shop
http://www.themapshop.co.uk

Amazon (French site) –
Suppliers of Club Vosgien maps
www.amazon.fr

Club Vosgien
publish maps and guides to the Vosges
www.club-vosgien.eu

Transport

SNCF French railways
www.sncf.com

Local buses, Montbéliard
www.montbeliard.fr/en-1-clic/bus.html

Local buses, Doubs
www.doubs.fr

APPENDIX E
Accommodation

GR5/GR53 Route: A web search will give up-to-date accommodation information, but the following selected contact details might help with planning.

Web links for gîtes and refuges
Refuges and gîtes
www.gites-refuges.com

Shelters
www.refuges.info

Amis de la Nature
(usually have restricted opening)
www.amis-nature.org

Club Vosgien
(usually have restricted opening)
www.club-vosgien.eu

Club Alpin Français
www.ffcam.fr

Section 1

Wissembourg
For hotels, see Wissembourg Tourist Office

Col du Pigeonnier
Refuge du Pigeonnier,
www.club-vosgien.eu

Climbach
À l'Ange (hotel)
tel 03 88 94 43 72
www.logishotels.com

Fleckenstein Camping
tel 03 88 94 40 38

Obersteinbach
Hotels, including Alsace-village
tel 03 88 09 50 59
www.alsace-village.com

Obersteinbach Gîte
tel 03 88 09 55 26

Windstein
Les Chambres d'Hôtes de Gabrielle
tel 03 88 09 24 41
www.gite-des-deux-chateaux.com

Hôtel du Windstein
tel 03 88 09 24 18
www.hotelduwindstein.com

Section 2

Niederbronn-les-Bains
For hotels, see Niederbronn-les-Bains Tourist Office

Heidenkopf (campsite)
www.camping-Niederbronn.eu

Lichtenberg
Hotels, including Au Soleil
tel 03 88 89 96 13
www.au-soleil-muhlheim.fr

Centre d'Accueil (gîte)
tel 03 88 89 96 06

Wimmenau
Hôtel à L'Aigle
tel 03 88 89 70 41
www.hotelrestaurantalaigle.com

La Petite-Pierre
For hotels, see La Petite-Pierre Tourist Office

Gîte d'étape de la Petite-Pierre
tel 03 88 01 47 00

Imsthal
Auberge d'Imsthal
tel 03 88 01 49 00

Graufthal
Au Vieux Moulin (hotel)
tel 03 88 70 17 28
www.auvieuxmoulin.eu

Section 3

Saverne
For hotels, see Saverne Tourist Office

Youth hostel
tel 03 88 91 14 84

La Hoube
Hôtel des Vosges
tel 03 87 08 80 44
www.hotel-restaurant-vosges.com

Dabo
Chalet du Rocher (gîte and campsite)
tel 03 87 07 47 51

Wangenbourg
For hotels, see Wangenbourg Tourist
Office

Refuge du Grand Tétras (gîte)
tel 03 88 87 34 34

Les Huttes (campsite)
www.camping-wangenbourg-engenthal.
com

Nideck
La Cascade de Nideck (gîte)
www.auberge-nideck.alsace

Gîte and campsite (Luttenbach)
tel 03 88 50 90 62

Urmatt
Hotels, including La Poste
tel 03 88 97 40 55
www.hotel-rest-laposte.fr

Col du Donon
Hotels, including Du Donon
tel 03 88 97 20 32
www.donon.fr

Wackenbach
Chambres d'hôtes, see Schirmeck
Tourist Office

Section 4

Rothau (nr Schirmeck)
La Claquette (hostel)
tel 03 88 97 06 08

Hôtel La Rubanerie
tel 03 88 97 01 95
www.larubanerie-hotel.com

La Serva (nr Champ du Feu)
Auberge and refuge Hazemann
tel 03 88 97 30 52
www.auberge-hazemann.com

Chaume des Veaux
La Chaume des Veaux (refuge)
www.amis-nature.org

Le Hohwald
For hotels, see Le Hohwald Tourist
Office

Le Hohwald (gîte)
tel 03 88 08 30 90

Mont Ste-Odile
Hotel (at convent)
tel 03 88 95 80 53
www.mont-sainte-odile.com

Barr
For hotels, see Barr Tourist Office

Foyer St Martin (campsite)
www.camping-foyer-saint-martin.fr

Mittelbergheim
Hotels, including Gilg
tel 03 88 08 91 37
www.hotel-gilg.com

Gruckert
Refuge du Gruckert
www.amis-nature.org

Reichsfeld
Domaine Bohn (chambre d'hôte)
tel 03 88 85 58 78
www.alsacehome.com

Châtenois
For hotels, see Châtenois Tourist Office

CCA (gîte)
tel 03 88 92 26 20
www.cca-chatenois.fr

Thannenkirch
Hotels, including Auberge de la
Meunière
tel 03 89 73 10 47
www.aubergelameuniere.com

Section 5

Ribeauvillé
For hotels, see Ribeauvillé Tourist Office

Col des Bagenelles
Chalet-Refuge du Col des Bagenelles
www.club-vosgien.eu

Le Bonhomme
Hotels, including La Poste
tel 03 89 47 51 10
www.hotel-la-poste.com

Les Myrtilles (campsite and gîte)
tel 03 89 47 57 50
www.lesmyrtilles68.com

Étang du Devin
L'Étang du Devin (hotel/gîte)
tel 03 89 47 20 29
www.etangdevin.com

Col du Calvaire
Les Terrasses du Lac Blanc (hotel)
tel 03 89 86 50 00
www.les-terrasses-du-lac-blanc.com

Centre Le Blancrupt (refuge)
tel 03 89 71 27 11
www.blancrupt.com

Schanzwasen
Auberge du Schantzwasen (hotel/
auberge)
tel 03 89 77 30 11
www.auberge-schanzwasen.com

Col de la Schlucht
Hôtel Du Chalet
tel 03 89 77 04 06
www.hotel-du-chalet.com

Trois-Fours
Chalet-Refuge des Trois-Fours
tel 03 89 77 32 59
www.ffcam.fr

Near Hohneck
Refuge du Sotré
tel 03 29 22 13 97
www.refugedusotre.com

Auberge au Pied du Hohneck
tel 03 29 63 11 50
www.le-pied-du-hohneck.com

Metzeral
Hotels, including Aux Deux Clefs
tel 03 89 77 61 48
www.aux-deux-clefs.com

Section 6

Mittlach
Les Rondins de la Fecht (chambres
d'hôtes)
tel 03 89 21 18 47
www.rondins-fecht.fr

Le Markstein
Hotels, including Wolf
tel 03 89 82 64 36
www.hotelwolf.info

Refuge Du Treh
www.amis-nature.org

Petit Chamois (gîte)
tel 03 89 38 25 92
gitepetitchamois.jimdo.com

Le Grand Ballon
Chalet-Hôtel du Grand Ballon
tel 03 89 48 77 99
www.chalethotel-grandballon.com

Molkenrain
Ferme-auberge du Molkenrain
tel 03 89 81 17 66
www.ferme-molkenrain.com

Refuge du Molkenrain
tel 03 89 37 32 52
www.amis-nature.org

Section 7

Thann
For hotels, see Thann Tourist Office

Cercle St-Thiébaut (gîte)
tel 03 89 37 59 60
www.cercle-thann.jimdo.com

Belacker
Gîte d'étape du Belaker
tel 06 30 08 11 26
www.belacker.fr

Near Col des Perches
Gazon Vert (gîte)
tel 09 88 18 71 65
www.gitedugazonvert.fr

Rouge Gazon (hotel/gîte)
tel 03 29 25 12 80
www.rouge-gazon.fr

Ballon d'Alsace
Grand Hôtel du Sommet
tel 03 84 29 30 60
www.hotelrestaurantdusommet.com

Malvaux
Auberge des Moraines
tel 03 84 26 37 14
www.auberge-les-moraines.eu

Giromagny
Le Paradis du Loups (hotel)
tel 03 84 26 64 25
www.leparadisdesloups.com

Relais du Randonneur (gîte)
tel 03 84 27 14 18

Lachapelle-sous-Chaux
Chambres d'hôtes, see Franche-Comté
Tourist Office website

Section 8

Héricourt
La Filature (hotel)
tel 03 84 56 80 80
www.la-filature.fr

Étupes
Hôtel Vielle Ferme
tel 03 81 32 21 75
www.la-vieille-ferme.fr

Audincourt/Montbéliard
For hotels, see Franche-Comté Tourist
Office website

Section 9

St-Hippolyte
For hotels, see St-Hippolyte Tourist
Office

Fessevillers
Fessevillers (gîte d'étape)
tel 03 81 44 40 35

Goumois
Hôtel Taillard
tel 03 81 44 20 75
www.hotel-taillard.fr

Bois de la Biche
Au Bois de la Biche (hotel)
tel 03 81 44 01 82
www.boisdelabiche.fr

Biaufond
Maison Biaufond
(hotel and refuge) (Switzerland)
tel 0041 (0) 32 968 60 60
www.maison-biaufond.ch

La Rasse
Hôtel Restaurant de la Rasse
tel 03 81 68 61 89
www.hoteldelarasse.com

Le Cerneux Billard
Gîte du Cerneux Billard
tel 09 61 31 66 57
gitecerneuxbillard.fr

Section 10

Villers-le-Lac
For hotels, see Villers-le-Lac Tourist
Office

Le Clos Rondot (gîte)
tel 06 81 70 51 84
www.leclosrondot.fr

Sur la Roche
Sur la Roche (auberge/gîte)
tel 03 81 68 08 94
www.auberge-surlaroche.com

Vieux Châteleu
Vieux Châteleu (auberge/gîte)
tel 03 81 67 11 59
www.chateleu.com

Les Gras
Chambres d'hôtes
tel 03 81 68 82 20
lamaisondesseignes.free.fr/

Les Alliés
Accueil nordique des Alliés (gîte)
tel 03 81 46 33 17

Pontarlier
For hotels, see Pontarlier Tourist Office

Les Fourgs
Chambres d'hôtes, see Franche-Comté
Tourist Office website

Les Granges Bailly (gîte)
tel 03 81 69 40 62

Section 11

Métabief
For hotels in Les Hôpitaux-Neufs and
Métabief see Métabief Tourist Office

Les Hôpitaux-Neufs
Le Miroir (campsite)
www.camping-lemiroir.com

Le Gros Morond
Chalet-Refuge du Gros Morond
tel 03 81 46 74 67
www.ffcam.fr

Mouthe
For chambres d'ôtes, see Mouthe Tourist
Office

Art et Randonnée (gîte)
tel 03 81 69 21 69

Chaux-Neuve
Auberge du Grand Git
tel 03 81 69 25 75
www.aubergedugrandgit.com

Chapelle-des-Bois
Hotels, including Les Bruyères
tel 03 81 69 21 71
www.hotellesbruyeres.fr

La Maison du Montagnon (gîte)
tel 03 81 69 26 30
www.maison-montagnon.eu

Chalet Gaillard (gîte)
tel 06 85 58 59 09
www.chaletgaillard.com

Les Rousses
For hotels, see Les Rousses Tourist Office

Le Grand Tétras (gîte)
tel 03 84 60 51 13
legrandtetras.troumad.org

La Cure
La Grenotte (gîte)
tel 03 84 60 54 82
www.lagrenotte.com

Hôtel Arbez Franco-Suisse
tel 03 84 60 02 20
www.logishotels.com

Chalet des Tuffes (gîte)
tel 03 84 45 58 62
www.ffcam.fr

La Givrine
La Givrine (hotel/gîte)
tel 0041 (0)22 360 11 1
www.restaurantdelagivrine.ch

St-Cergue
For hotels, see St-Cergue Tourist Office

Nyon
For hotels, see Nyon Tourist Office